Perspectives on the Uniform Commercial Code

Perspectives on the Uniform Commercial Code

Douglas Litowitz

CAROLINA ACADEMIC PRESS
Durham, North Carolina

ISBN: 0-89089-630-5
LCCN: 2001089664

Carolina Academic Press
700 Kent Street
Durham, North Carolina 27701
Telephone (919) 489-7486
Fax (919) 493-5668
www.cap-press.com

Printed in the United States of America

Contents

Preface

This book is a supplemental teaching tool for courses on the Uniform Commercial Code (the "Code"). The readings in this book refute the widely held belief that commercial law is boring and mechanical.

This book is also a reaction to the traditional method of teaching commercial law. Virtually without exception, professors of commercial law eschew outside readings that might raise broader ethical and conceptual questions about the Code. Instead, they require students to purchase only a casebook and a statutory supplement. Class sessions are typically devoted solely to mastering and applying various provisions of the Code, with no attention paid to the history and controversies that surrounded the Code and its enactment, amendment, and enforcement. The results have been predictable: students treat the Code precisely as they find it presented in the classroom—a static and apolitical monolith that is not worthy of outside discussion. And so we find that our students typically emerge from courses in commercial law with a grudging respect for the Code but with little understanding of its place within the larger framework of American law. The readings in this book should provide a broader and more humanistic backdrop for the Code, allowing students to see that commercial law (just like constitutional law and administrative law) raises important moral and political questions of its own. At the very least, students will understand that the Code is an ongoing construction that mediates between competing social, political, and economic interests.

The readings in this book are deliberately short, in part to match the attention span of a typical (that is, busy) law student. The original texts have been edited mercilessly to focus attention on one or two key issues at the expense of all the other issues raised by the authors, so readers are encouraged to consult the full articles for a more complete treatment. In choosing the selections for this book, I have drawn heavily from classic texts on the Code, supplementing these readings with a few cutting-edge selections. In addition to editing for content, I have omitted footnotes to provide for greater readability, and I have included only a single discussion question following each reading.

This book can be integrated into the standard commercial law course without much difficulty. I suggest that professors assign the Introduction and the first two chapters as background reading prior to the first day of class, to give students a conceptual and historical overview of the Code. Once the course has begun, I suggest that every other class period, one or more students should be assigned to present a selection to the class, capping the presentation by answering the discussion question following the selection. A ten-minute session during alternating class periods will likely suffice to instill a more comprehensive understanding of the Code without making the book seem an intrusion into traditional Code pedagogy. Additionally, this book can be used as a device for assigning extra credit to students who take the time to prepare short opinion pieces assessing the selections.

Karl Llewellyn, the principal architect of the Code, once wrote that the Code stood a good chance of adoption by the several states because its subject matter (namely, transactions involving personal property and payments) was "very largely non-political in character." This claim was untrue when it was made, and has become even less credible over time, especially in an intellectual climate where legal scholars rightfully view every area of law as an inherently contested and political arena for engaging in social construction. To the extent that law shapes social ontology and constrains legal actors by allocating benefits and burdens, every arrangement of law is an active *choice* among many possible worlds, each with its own moral, political, and economic landscape. The same is true for the Code—it does not merely hover above a pre-existing world of commercial practices, but represents a commitment to bring a particular commercial world into existence. As the default architecture for commercial practices, the Code is infinitely contestable and subject to constant adjustment. Yet despite its dynamic character, the Code often appears to students as a closed text that could not assume any other form. Therefore, we need to guard against reifying the Code as a final, totalizing document, and instead see it as a social construction that can be *decon*structed in the interests of justice. This book is intended as an initial step toward creating a generation of law students who are not content with merely mastering the Code, but who are capable of thinking critically about it.

* * *

All of my work, including this project, draws upon the strength and encouragement of my parents Bonnie and Norman Litowitz, and my brothers Alec and Malcolm. Through countless discussions spanning a series of difficult years, they redirected my negative energy into positive channels and encouraged the pursuit of my intellectual vision, despite an interminable parade of relocations, disappointments, and institutional absurdities. Unfortunately, there was one member of my family who did not live to see the completion of this project, and that was my grandmother Betty Litowitz, with whom I lived while assembling the book. A complicated woman who was by turns maddening and hilarious, she will forever live inside of me. This book is dedicated to her, and also to the memory of Dr. Ralph Leischner, the father of my sister-in-law Jennifer and a pillar of our extended family. He will be missed by more people in more ways than it would be possible to mention.

Finally, thanks to the lovely Vicki Chen of Savannah, Georgia, for designing the original book cover.

Douglas Litowitz

Jacksonville, FL
December 2000

Introduction for Law Students

You are probably reading this book because you are a law student who is taking a course on the Uniform Commercial Code (the "Code"). If so, this will be one of three books assigned by your professor—the other two books are a casebook and a statutory supplement. The casebook will introduce you to various provisions of the Code and it will supply hypothetical problems that you will attempt to solve using the Code. The statutory supplement contains the full text of the Code and related statutes. The purpose of the book that you are holding is to give you a broader understanding of the history, evolution, and overall philosophy of the Code. Toward that end, this Introduction will get you started with a very brief guide to the Code, a picture that will become clearer throughout the semester.

Let's start with each of the words in the phrase *Uniform Commercial Code*. The word *Uniform* signifies that the Code is a model law that was drafted by experts who sought to have the same set of provisions adopted in every state. Similar uniform acts would include the Uniform Probate Code and the Uniform Partnership Act. Like all uniform statutes, the version of the Code in your statutory supplement is not "the law" unless and until it gets enacted by a state legislature. Luckily, most states have enacted the entire model version of the Code without shocking alterations, so in large measure the Code lives up to the word *Uniform*: a given Code section is likely to be the same in Illinois, Florida, Texas, Kansas, etc. You should be aware, however, that some states made significant non-uniform changes to the Code before enacting it into law, a process that is discouraged because it destroys uniformity of the Code from state-to-state. It would perhaps be more accurate for law students to study the specific version of the Code that was enacted in the state where they intend to practice law, but since law professors have no way of knowing where students will end up, the safest tactic is to teach the model version of the Code, and to let students pick up the idiosyncratic state deviations when they begin practicing law. So when your professor refers to the Uniform Commercial Code, you may assume that she is referencing the model statute contained in your statutory supplement, which may differ slightly from the version enacted in your state.

The word *Commercial* designates that the subject matter of the Code is commercial transactions, namely transactions dealing with personal (moveable) property and payments. Such transactions include the sale, lease, consignment, transport, storage, and granting of security interests in goods as collateral, as well as payments in the form of promissory notes, checks, and wire transfers (plus investment securities as well). In terms of the persons brought within the Code, you should know that the Code covers transactions by businesses and individuals alike, from gigantic department stores and national banks all the way down to door-to-door sales and rental car leases. In fact, the Code covers many transactions that affect your life on a daily basis, including the products and food that you buy, the car that you lease, the furniture that you buy on credit, the checks that you write, and the promissory note which you signed for your student loan, just to name a few transactions.

The word *Code* designates that the Code is a unified and coherent statute which was intended to cover the entire field of commercial law. Remember that a *code* is different from a *statute* in much the same way that a pair of pants is different from a patch sewn over one of the knees: while both are legislative enactments, a *code* is an internally consistent series of provisions that creates a total framework for an area of law, while a *statute* merely regulates one aspect of an area that is already governed by common law. The Code is not a piecemeal statute that remedies a problem area within the general law of contracts (for example, many states have special laws regulating the sale of health club memberships, thereby supplementing the general law of contracts that would otherwise govern such transactions). Instead of merely supplementing the law of contracts, the Code covers the entire area of commercial law, from the formation of a contract to remedies for breach. When a dispute breaks out over a commercial transaction, the Code is the first place to check, and the common law of contracts will be relevant only if the Code permits us to consult it. Naturally, courts have interpreted the Code in various ways, and therefore it is necessary for lawyers to consult not only the Code but also the case law decided under it. Still, there is significance in the fact that the Code takes the form of a unified *code* and not merely a *statute*: it means that you will be spending lots of time moving from one Code provision to another, and spending less time on case decisions.

Now that you understand the term *Uniform Commercial Code*, you will need to understand the Code's place within the framework of American legal history. Simply put, the Code project was the most ambitious attempt at codification in American legal history: It began in the early 1940s and led to a final draft of the Code in the early 1950s, although the Code was not widely enacted until the 1960s. The Code project was a joint effort by two organizations that had long been trying to clarify and unify American law: the National Conference of Commissioners on Uniform State Laws (NCCUSL) and the American Law Institute (ALI). Prior to the Code project, the NCCUSL had produced a series of uniform acts, and the ALI had produced the *Restatements*. To this day, both organizations remain actively involved with the Code.

The Code project began as an attempt to put in one place all of the relevant laws concerning commercial transactions and payments. To understand why this was thought to be a pressing need, remember that American law followed the common law tradition inherited from England, where precedent-setting decisions are built up like grains of sand until they form a coherent body of law. By the latter half of the Nineteenth Century, commercial law was largely non-statutory and developing piecemeal from state to state. This arrangement proved deeply problematic for business enterprises (banks, corporations, finance companies, manufacturers) because it created a patchwork quilt of unstable law. For example, a national bank might use a standard-form promissory note that was enforceable in one state but unenforceable in the neighboring state. This would require the bank to wade through the law of each state and adjust its standard-forms accordingly, thereby raising legal costs that were passed onto customers. So there were two key problems that the drafters of the Code wanted to fix. First, the law of commercial transactions was an uncertain mixture of case decisions and occasional statutes, and second, commercial law was not uniform from state to state. On a more abstract level, there was a growing concern that the increasingly fast-paced world of commercial transactions in America could no longer be governed by the old English rules of contract law, with its rigid requirements of offer/acceptance, consideration, writing requirements, the 'mailbox rule,' and so forth.

For a long time, the solution was thought to lie in convincing each state to adopt a predetermined package of uniform laws covering the same subareas within commercial law—one statute for sales, one for negotiable instruments, and so forth. This was the approach that the NCCUSL took during the late Nineteenth Century and early Twentieth Century, as it churned out a series of uniform laws with the hope that the same package of laws would be adopted by all of the states, creating *de facto* uniformity. This plan didn't work. Not all states adopted the same uniform laws, and many did so with changes, creating another patchwork of inconsistent laws from state to state. Another possible solution explored at this time was the enactment of federal law governing commercial transactions, which would ensure uniformity by virtue of federal supremacy over state law. For reasons that will become clear in the following chapter, this solution failed as well. So as late as the 1940s, the law of commercial transactions was piecemeal, fragmentary, and non-uniform among the states. This didn't stop commercial transactions from taking place, but business persons were rightfully skittish since the law was inconsistent across state lines, and it still reflected common law principles of contract law that were increasingly outdated.

Ultimately the Code was hit upon as the solution—a gigantic uniform law encompassing and supplanting all of the prior uniform laws, to be adopted whole cloth by each state, thereby ensuring the two magic ingredients sought by business enterprises, namely a modern statement of the law in statutory format, plus uniformity among jurisdictions. The idea behind the Code was to put in one location all of the laws relevant to a commercial transaction, thereby condensing, simplifying, and modernizing the entire area of law. A major impetus was to create a legal framework that could evolve to reflect changing commercial practices in the marketplace instead of conforming to the strictures and formalities of black-letter contract law. After reading the selections in this book, you will be able to judge for yourself whether the Code project has been a success.

You should now open your statutory supplement and spend about two minutes skimming the very short "General Comment" preceding the text of the Uniform Commercial Code. This General Comment was written by the NCCUSL and the ALI, the two groups that sponsored the Code project and which remain responsible for it. The General Comment briefly explains the reasons why the Code was created and it lists the uniform acts which the Code was intended to replace (it also lists most of the key players involved in the financing and drafting of the Code). After reading the General Comment, you should spend a few minutes leafing through the text of the Code so that it becomes less mysterious. To get a feel for how the Code works, I suggest that you turn to section 2-202 (the parole evidence rule for contracts involving the sale of goods) and compare this version of the parole evidence rule with the version that you learned in your first-year Contracts course.

Now turn to the table of contents in your statutory supplement. You will notice that the Uniform Commercial Code consists of a series of Articles dealing with different areas of commercial law; together the Articles take up approximately the first half of the statutory supplement. The subsequent one-quarter of the statutory supplement consists of prior versions and proposed amendments of various Articles; these are included to show you how the Code has been amended in the past and how it will likely be amended in the future. You should know that each time the model version of the Code is amended by the NCCUSL and the ALI, the amendments are then brought up for adoption in each state legislature.

If you glance at the remaining material in your statutory supplement, you will see a long list of uniform acts, federal laws, and federal regulations. These have all been included because the Code is not capable of standing on its own as the single source for all laws governing commercial transactions. Take a brief look at these supplemental materials and you will notice a series of uniform state laws that have been enacted by various states to complement or modify the provisions of the Code (for example, your statutory supplement probably contains the Uniform Consumer Credit Code, which has been enacted in a small number of states to provide greater consumer protection than the Code). Apart from these uniform state laws, you will see a long list of federal statutes and regulations that apply to commercial transactions. These statutes represent an attempt by the federal government to preempt inconsistent Code provisions (which are state law) by virtue of the supremacy clause of the Constitution. For example, your supplement will contain the Magnuson-Moss Warranty Act, a federal law that is more strict than the Code on the labeling of warranties. All of this material is supplemental to the Code but it is nevertheless important because it demonstrates that the Code is not the sole source of law for commercial transactions, which means that the diligent lawyer must also consult outside statutes at the state and federal levels. Rest assured that your course will focus primarily upon the text of the Code itself, passing to supplemental materials only when you are discussing Code provisions that have been affected by outside laws.

You are now ready to begin your journey into the Code. Let me remind you that many (perhaps most) lawyers see the Code as a blunt instrument to be mechanically applied to conflicts that arise in commercial settings. Such people can become quite adept at making their way through the Code, just as a builder can become adept with a hammer yet have no appreciation for architecture. But without a deeper comprehension of the philosophy, structure, and methodology of the Code, such people are not capable of formulating policy arguments and interpretations that pass beyond mere 'Code-crunching.' The first step toward getting a deeper understanding of the Code is to place it in historical perspective, which is the topic of Chapter One.

Perspectives on the Uniform Commercial Code

Chapter One

Commercial Law before the Code

This chapter provides a historical overview of commercial law in general and the Uniform Commercial Code (the "Code") in particular.

In the first selection, Charles Bane provides a marvelously clear account of the evolution of commercial law from the medieval period to the present. He identifies five stages of commercial law:

(1) The era of the 'law merchant,' when disputes were settled on the spot according to customs prevailing among merchants (approximately 1300s–1700s);

(2) the era of the great English common law judges Holt and Mansfield, who tried to integrate the law merchant into the common law (the 1700s);

(3) the reception of English law in the American colonies via Blackstone's *Commentaries* and the attempt by Justice Story to create uniformity in the law of commercial transactions (1800s);

(4) the attempt by the National Conference of Commissioners on Uniform State Laws (NCCUSL) and the American Law Institute (ALI) to unify and modernize the law by promulgating uniform acts and the *Restatements* (1890s–1940s); and

(5) the creation of the Code by the NCCUSL and the ALI, and its widespread adoption by the states (1940–1960s).

In the second selection, William Twining (noted biographer of Karl Llewellyn, the principal architect of the Code), explains in detail how the Code emerged from the joint efforts of the NCCUSL and the ALI. Of particular historical interest is the fact that the Code project drew much of its intensity from the abandonment of efforts to enact a federal law governing the sale of goods. As we will see in Chapter Six, the possibility of 'federalizing' commercial law remains attractive to commercial lawyers as a possible method for ensuring uniformity among the states in the area of commercial law.

In the final selection, Professor Dennis Patterson discusses two radical ideas from Karl Llewellyn, the first of which made it into the Code while the second was abandoned. The first idea was Llewellyn's rejection of the formalism that haunted contract law (i.e., the insistence that a contract satisfy formal requirements such as the mirroring of offer/acceptance, consideration, the obsession with questions of title, strict rules on writing requirements, and so forth). In reaction to this, Llewellyn opted for an expansive concept of "Agreement" codified in 1-201(3) of the Code, which allowed binding agreements to be formed on the basis of customs prevailing in the commercial community. Llewellyn's second idea, which did *not* find a home in the Code, was that specialized merchant-juries should be used instead of civil juries to determine the operative merchant customs in commercial cases. As a matter of intellectual genealogy, Patterson links Llewellyn to the great Twentieth Century philosopher Ludwig Wittgenstein, who insisted that meanings were tied to social practices and forms of life. Llewellyn broke with traditional contract law by insisting that the true meaning of a contract was not limited to the formal words on paper or the intentions within the parties' heads, but to the overall commercial context. Patterson's important message about Llewellyn's philosophies may appear somewhat abstract at this juncture, but it will become increasingly cogent as you see how the Code departs from the formalism that you studied in your Contracts course.

The Progressive Development of Commercial Law
Charles Bane[1]

The earliest recorded judicial institution that determined issues of commercial law was the piepowder court, which made its appearance in England in the middle of the thirteenth century and existed for more than three centuries thereafter to settle disputes between merchants. English society in the thirteenth century was rural and agrarian; what trade there was took place at local fairs. The piepowder courts were established at these fairs; their name evolved from an Anglicization of the Norman-French term "pie poudres," meaning powdered or dirty feet and referring to the shoes of the itinerant merchants who traded goods at the fairs. The authority to hold a

---

1. Charles Bane, The Progressive Development of Commercial Law, 37 U. Miami L. Rev. 351 (1983). Copyright 1983 by the University of Miami. Reprinted by permission.

piepowder court was part of the royal franchise to a lord or borough to hold a fair. Court was held before the lord's stewart of the market, or if it was a borough fair, before the mayor or bailiff of the borough. The court's jurisdiction was confined to disputes arising at the fair; this included matters of debt, contract, trespass, and violations of the Assizes of Bread and Beer. The proceedings were held in a shed and were highly informal, probably resembling more a street corner argument than a modern trial. It was justice on the spot, with no delays. In Colchester in 1458, a merchant-creditor sued in a piepowder court at eight o'clock in the morning to recover a debt. He won a default judgment at noon and attached the debtor's goods by four o'clock that afternoon.

The piepowder courts applied rules of decision derived from the customs and usages of the merchants. These rules became known at the law merchant. In accordance with the law merchant, the piepowder courts enforced informal oral and written agreements at a time when the common law courts, bound by the forms of action, were enforcing only written agreements under seal.

As trade and commerce began to expand beyond the local fairs, merchants looked for more efficient alternatives to the piepowder courts. The results was the Statute of the Staple, promulgated in 1353 and described as the most important of all medieval English commercial statutes. The Statute established courts in fifteen staple towns in England, Ireland, and Wales, which became known as Courts of the Staple. The mayor of the staple town, along with two constables, presided over the court and exercised jurisdiction over all matters relating to the staple. The Statute required the mayor to have knowledge of the law merchant and expressly provided that the staple courts were to apply the law merchant and not common law. The juries that were used were composed exclusively of merchants. One staple court lawsuit was based on a claim that wool delivered was not true to the sale sample; jurisdiction was held to rest in the staple court because sales by sample were regulated according to the custom of merchants—the law merchant...

When Sir Edward Coke became Chief Justice of the King's Bench in 1613, the common-law courts began to assert a general jurisdiction over commercial matters—at the expense of the jurisdiction of the piepowder and staple courts. A new pleading practice sprang up in the common-law courts in the 1600's which urged that prevailing customs among merchants could be the basis for a legal duty. The pleadings alleged the custom, the facts of the case, and that the rights and duties of the parties arose by virtue of the custom. [But still, the substantive rules of the law merchant were not integrated into the common law; instead the law merchant was considered a set of customary practices that could be introduced in cases decided under the general principles of the common law].

In the eighteenth century two renowned common-law judges, Lord John Holt and Lord Mansfield, turned their talents to the law merchant. [U]nder these two judges, the law merchant was integrated into the common law of England.

The first of these two innovators came to the King's Bench in 1689 and held office until shortly before his death in 1710. Under Holt, the common law courts, when hearing commercial cases, began to take judicial notice of some of the more notable mercantile customs. For those cases in which he did not take judicial notice of a particular mercantile custom, Holt often used the ancient institution of the special jury, composed of merchants, to advise him on mercantile customs in England's rapidly developing trade and commerce activities. Once, he invited all prominent London merchants to advise him on a question concerning acceptance of a bill of exchange.

Although Holt was innovative in most areas of commercial law, he was often conservative in some of the relatively new areas of trade and commerce. For example, Holt refused to accept the seventeenth-century mercantile custom that recognized promissory notes as negotiable instruments. The was intolerable for English bankers and merchants. In 1704 they succeeded in having promulgated the Promissory Notes Act, which made promissory noted assignable in the same manner as inland bills of exchange.

The second eighteenth-century judge who contributed to the development of commercial law needed no parliamentary impetus to effect reforms. Lord Mansfield was born as William Murray in 1706 into the Scottish peerage and served as Chief Justice of the King's Bench from 1756 to 1788. His contribution to commercial law is immeasurable—it prepared English law for the Industrial Revolution and its reforms.

Mansfield took decisive action to bring the law merchant into the common law. His primary technique was to use a special jury of merchants to find the appropriate mercantile custom or usage and then to use that finding as a rule of law for subsequent cases. Mansfield used the special jury to create a channel of communication between the judge and merchant. He treated his corps with respect and dignity, and he often invited them to dine with him. Each of them in turn regarded it as an honor to be one of Lord Mansfield's jurymen. Businessmen found they could obtain speedy justice before the King's Bench because of Mansfield's efficiency and diligence. Commercial cases flowed into his court, almost draining rival courts. Mansfield's zeal sometimes led him to hold court on holidays, when courts would customarily adjourn. At one session Mansfield announced his intention of sitting on Good Friday, which prompted Sergeant Davy, a prominent lawyer, to remark that "Your Lordship will be the first judge to have done so since Pontius Pilate." Mansfield [is now considered to be a leading figure in commercial law owing to] his views on the necessity of upholding the negotiability of bills of exchange and promissory notes...

Sir William Blackstone's treatment of the law merchant in his famous *Commentaries* is unsatisfactory, considering that he was living and writing in the eighteenth century during a time of great developments in commercial law. In late editions of the *Commentaries*, when Mansfield's work was nearly done, Blackstone devoted only five pages to bills of exchange (which he said were commonly known as drafts) and promissory notes, under the rubric of "debts upon simple contract." He covered sales in only six pages, under "contract," but devoted several pages to the almost obsolete market overt.

It is surprising that Blackstone ignored Mansfield's work, for the two men were contemporaries who knew and respected each other. Blackstone had praised Mansfield's work in prize cases, and Mansfield had supported Blackstone for the Vinerian Professorship at Oxford University where Blackstone delivered the lectures that were to form the basis for his *Commentaries*. Perhaps Blackstone was simply unaware of the efforts of Mansfield and Holt to incorporate the law merchant into the common law. Blackstone regarded the law merchant not as a part of the common law, but as part of the law of nations [international law] and enforced in England as such [probably because the law merchant arose from international fairs and markets during the medieval period]...

As part of the British Empire, the American colonies had, of course, been subject to the English common law, and by extension, the law merchant. [After the American revolution] the thirteen new United States moved quickly to adopt the English common law as the foundation for the law of their respective states. The law merchant was considered to be a part of the common law within the meaning of the reception statutes. The reception statutes were the mechanism for transferring the common law of England to the new United States, but for the contents of that common law, American lawyers relied heavily on Blackstone's *Commentaries*. All editions, and especially the 1783 edition, were widely circulated in the United States.

America's expanding commercial activities precluded a rote reliance on Blackstone's work, for Blackstone gave only cursory treatment to the law merchant. The United States in the early part of the nineteenth century had no national currency; private bank notes were the medium of exchange. Bills of exchange were widely used as commercial instruments, especially in the East. Promissory notes were everywhere and people were quite familiar with the basic rules on endorsements. The courts carefully preserved the fundamental virtue of these instruments: their negotiability. But new mercantile customs were springing up in America that did not fit easily into the English law merchant. American courts, however, could not emulate Mansfield's technique for incorporating a mercantile custom in the common law. American trade, spread out over several states, was varied and diverse, whereas Mansfield's commercial class was insulated and homogeneous. A Justice of the United States Supreme Court believed he had an answer to this confusion: codification.

A remarkably industrious man, Joseph Story carried on four professions at the same time: Justice of the United States Supreme Court, Professor of Law at Harvard University, President of the Bank of Salem (in Massachusetts), and author of nine legal treatises. Two of the treatises, *Commentaries on the Law of Bills of Exchange* and *Commentaries on the Law of Promissory Notes*, comprised the first comprehensive study of American negotiable instruments.

Justice Story, anticipating many great commercial law scholars, believed commercial law should be codified. Not content to simply suggest a codification of American commercial law, Story tried to develop some uniformity in judicial treatment of commercial matters by creating a federal law merchant. In *Swift v. Tyson* (1842), a diversity action involving a bill of exchange, the issue was whether a preexisting debt was valid consideration for the bill. The defendant-acceptor contended that under the law of New York, where the bill was accepted, it was. Writing for the Court, Story first determined that New York law was not binding on the Supreme Court. Story held that as a matter of *federal common law*, a preexisting debt could not be a valid consideration for the bill.

Codification of American commercial law, despite the efforts of Justice Story, was not to occur for another fifty years. An then came not through the rickety federal law merchant developed under the ill-fated *Swift v. Tyson*, but by uniform statutes enacted by the states. [*Swift v. Tyson* was overruled by *Erie R.R. v. Tompkins*, 304 U.S. 64 (1938), which rejected Story's notion of a federal common law of commercial transactions].

The need for modernization and codification of commercial law was perhaps greatest in the law of bills of exchange and promissory noted. Bills and notes were the oil for running the American business machine, but they generated almost endless possibilities for disputes. Courts were clogged with questions of negotiability and transfer. In the *Century Edition of the American Digest,* covering cases up to 1896, the subject of bills and notes took up virtually one entire volume of more than 2,700 pages.

Given the confusion of the law of bills and notes, it is not surprising that the first uniform law was the Negotiable Instruments Law, drafted under the auspices of an organization now known as the National Conference of Commissioners on Uniform State Laws (NCCUSL). The Conference was organized at the urging of the American Bar Association and held its first meeting in 1892. Commissioners were in attendance from Delaware, Georgia, Massachusetts, Michigan, New York, New Jersey, and Pennsylvania. One of first actions of this initial conference was to recommend uniform state legislation that would (1) abolish days of grace on all bills and notes, and (2) provide that all bills and notes falling due on a Sunday or legal holiday should be payable and presentable on the next following secular or business day. These were matters of great concern to bankers and merchants who, it was said, could "never be certain on what day commercial paper...is really due if made payable without the State."

The commissioners at the 1895 conference authorized their Committee on Commercial Law to prepare a draft of a uniform statute on commercial paper, based upon an English statute on the same subject. The final draft of the statute, eventually known as the Uniform Negotiable Instruments Act, was approved by the Commissioners at their sixth conference in 1896. Through the efforts of the Commissioners, the Act was subsequently adopted by all of the states, territories, and insular possessions of the United States. The Act has been judicially recognized as a codification of the law merchant; section 196 of the Act stated, "In any case not provided for in this act the rules of the law merchant shall govern." One purpose of this provision was stated in the Commissioners' note to the section: "to leave room for the growth of new usages and customs so that none of these acts should put the law merchant in a straightjacket and thus prevent the further expansion of the law merchant."

In the early 1900's, the NCCUSL authorized the preparation of four more uniform acts. Professor Samuel Williston drafted all four: Sales (1906), Warehouse Receipts (1906), Bills of Lading (1909), and Stock Transfers (1909). These acts received wide acceptance by the states, though none matched the popularity of the Uniform Negotiable Instruments Act.

In 1940, William A. Schnader, President of the NCCUSL, spoke at the Conference's 50th Annual Meeting. He noted that there had been substantial changes in methods of transacting business since the approval of previous uniform acts and that many of these acts had been adopted piecemeal. Schnader focused on the duplication and inconsistencies in the provisions governing negotiable instruments, bills of lading, warehouse receipts, stock transfers, sales, and trust receipts. He recommended against attempts to revise and update the individual acts, which would have required 371 separate legislative battles. Instead, he advocated the preparation of "a great uniform commercial code...which would bring the commercial law up to date, and which could become the uniform law of our fifty-three jurisdictions, by the passage of only fifty-three acts, instead of many times that number." This was the genesis of the Uniform Commercial Code.

On the day following Schnader's address, Karl N. Llewellyn, Chairman of the Uniform Commercial Acts Section of the NCCUSL, presented his Section's report to the NCCUSL. Llewellyn, a professor of law at Columbia University, had been drafting as Reporter (expert draftsman) for a revised Uniform Sales Act. He reported that the revised Sales Act was being drafted so that it could be a separate uniform act or a chapter in a possible uniform commercial code. Before the meeting concluded, the Executive Committee had approved "the preparation of a Commercial Code...as soon as funds are available in an amount deemed by the Executive Committee to be adequate."

There was some urgency about the project. The Merchants Association of New York City was pressing for federal commercial legislation following the 1938 United States Supreme Court decision in *Erie R.R. v. Tompkins*, which overruled *Swift v. Tyson*. The New York merchants were not alone in regarding *Erie* as foreclosing any possibility of achieving a uniform commercial law through the federal courts. But the disruption of World War II and an initial difficulty in raising funds slowed progress on the commercial code. Nevertheless, the revised Uniform Sales Act was completed in 1944. That same year, the Maurice and Laura Falk Foundation made the first of its generous grants, eventually totaling $250,000, for the commercial code project.

Work on the Code began in earnest in 1945 as a cooperative effort of the NCCUSL and the American Law Institute (ALI). They were committed to completing it within five years. Karl Llewellyn served as Chief Reporter for the entire project, with Soia Mentschikoff as Associate Chief Reporter. Drafting proceeded at full speed with an editorial board reviewing progress throughout the year. At least once a year the entire NCCUSL and the ALI reviewed the drafts. Preliminary copies of Code sections were also submitted for comment to a special Uniform Commercial Code Committee of the American Bar Association Corporate Law Section. The Reporters sought advice from state and local bar associations and consulted with lay advisors from various associations or groups of merchants, businessmen, bankers, warehouse operators, and farmers. These efforts culminated in 1951, when the NCCUSL, the ALI, and the American Bar Association House of Delegates approved the completed Code.

The NCCUSL and the ALI debated whether the Code should be presented to Congress for enactment; indeed, the Code was drafted so that it could have been suited for national legislation with only a few changes. But the sponsoring organizations concluded that congressional enactment would be only a partial remedy; it was doubtful that federal authority over interstate commerce would reach the multitudinous commercial transactions covered by the Code. Further, the Commissioners, dedicated to uniform *state* laws, were biased in favor of state enactment. The sponsors then considered an attempt to achieve uniform state enactment through an interstate compact, but concluded that there were no advantages to this method over legislative enactments by the individual states.

The leadership of the NCCUSL pressed on for individual state enactment, concentrating first on the larger, more commercially active states, but with the ultimate goal of enactment by all states—thus bringing under the Code all commercial transactions within the nation. The Code was introduced in 1953 in the legislatures of several states, including: California, Mississippi, and New York, ostensibly for educational purposes. Under the prodding of William Schnader, Pennsylvania enacted the Code in 1953 without a single dissenting vote.

Objections developed. Some consumer advocates characterized the Code as "lawyers and bankers relief act" and objected to the absence of consumer credit protections. Certain New York bankers strongly objected to the Code, and when it was introduced in New York in 1953, the legislators sent it to the New York Law Revision Committee for comment and analysis. The Commission spent three years in hearings; the Code's editorial board followed every hearing, and drafted amendments to meet objections and explained why others were unnecessary. The result was the *Uniform Commercial Code— 1957 Official Edition...*

The Conference made available to legislatures a team of experts (Llewellyn, Mentschikoff, and University of Wisconsin law professor Charles Bunn, who helped edit the final version of the Code) to answer questions about the Code. Largely through their efforts, and the efforts of the Commissioners, Massachusetts adopted the Code in 1957; Kentucky in 1958; Connecticut and New Hampshire in 1959; seven states, including the large commercial states of Ohio, Illinois, and New Jersey in 1961; New York in 1962; and so on until all states [except Louisiana] were in line by 1967.

Discussion Question: Bane begins the historical overview with the law merchant, which continues to hold a particular fascination for commercial lawyers, since it delivered speedy justice according to the customs prevailing among merchants. Take a look at the reference to the law merchant as a supplemental source of law for the Code (section 1-103); then look at how the Code seeks to encompass changing customs and practices (section 1-102(2)(b)); and then see how the term "Agreement" is defined in 1-201(3) to include "usage of trade" (1-205). This should indicate that the Code has adopted the spirit of the law merchant by allowing courts to look at the practices within the marketplace as forming part of the parties' contract. This differs sharply from black-letter contract law, which does not incorporate the changing customs of merchants. Do you see any problems with incorporating customs and practices into the Code? Does it make the Code flexible and contemporary, or does it merely allow the law to uncritically reflect the status quo of industry practices?

The Genesis of the Uniform Commercial Code
William Twining[2]

The story of the Uniform Commercial Code has its roots in the history of two national institutions, the NCCUSL and the ALI. Both of these came into being in response to the need for unification, simplification and betterment of law in the United States. The NCCUSL was founded, largely, on the initiative of the American Bar Association, in 1892. From the outset the NCCUSL consisted of unpaid commissioners appointed by the governors of the states; up to 1940 it had rarely met more than once a year and for the most part it had restricted its activities to preparing and promulgating acts which it recommended for adoption to the legislatures of the various states. Over a long period of time it was conspicuously successful in securing the wide adoption of uniform statutes relating to commercial law [such as the Negotiable Instruments Law and the Uniform Sales Act].

Although by 1940 seven major uniform acts had over time been adopted by a substantial majority of American jurisdictions, in some cases by all of them, the process had been extremely slow and laborious. For instance, it had never taken less than ten years between the date of promulgation of an act and its adoption by a majority of the states; it took forty-seven years to secure the enactment in every jurisdiction of the Uniform Stock Transfer Act, promulgated in 1909; after fifty years only thirty-four states had enacted the Uniform Sales Act. Further difficulties arose when the conference proposed amendments. For example, although all jurisdictions enacted the Uniform Warehouse Receipts Act, even as late as 1958 only sixteen had adopted the amendments proposed by the conference in 1922. Thus up to 1940 the NCCUSL had not satisfactorily resolved the problem

2. William Twining, Karl Llewellyn and the Realist Movement (Norman: University of Oklahoma Press, 1973). Reprinted by permission.

of reconciling the need for uniformity with the need for continuous improvement and adaption to changing conditions.

The ALI has its origins in a project for a 'juristic center for the betterment of the law' that was proposed by members of the Association of American Law Schools in 1921. An extremely distinguished committee of forty, under the chairmanship of Elihu Root, was established in 1921 and reported in 1922. The report of the committee is over one hundred pages long and it contains what is still one of the best orthodox analyses of the major contending forces at work in promoting and fighting uncertainty, complexity and lack of uniformity in American Law. The main recommendations of the committee were that the American Law Institute should be set up and that its first major undertaking should be to prepare a 'Restatement of the Law'...

The creation of the Uniform Commercial Code represents one phase in the history of the struggles of various national organizations with the intractable problems of unification, simplification and modernization of law in the United States. The project has its immediate roots in a number of attempts to remedy deficiencies in the Uniform Sales Act. This Act was adopted by the NCCUSL in 1906 and by 1937 had been enacted in over thirty jurisdictions. The first important impetus for revision came from the movement to introduce a federal sales act, applicable to inter-state and foreign transactions. In 1922 a committee of the American Bar Association produced a draft Federal Sales Bill which contained modifications of and additions to the Uniform Sales Act. This particular bill made little headway in Congress. In January 1937, Congressman Walter Chandler of Tennessee introduced a new bill, in the House of Representatives. This bill followed the Uniform Sales Act very closely. Widespread interest was stimulated. The most significant response came from the Merchants' Association of New York, which set up a committee to study the bill. Their report, which was published in February 1937, supported the introduction of a Federal Sales Act as an instrument of unification, but suggested some amendments which would lead to significant departures from the Uniform Sales Act. The bill was re-drafted in the light of this report. This embodied nearly all of the proposals of the Merchants Association and was introduced in Congress by Chandler in July 1937. It was referred to the Committee on Interstate and Foreign Commerce, where it died. However, it was resuscitated two years later by Representative Herron Pearson of Tennessee. In the interim there had been considerable activity. In 1937 the ABA had adopted a resolution urging the enactment of such a bill; in 1939 the American Association of Law Schools devoted a round table to the bill and this formed the basis of a symposium published in the March 1940 issue of the *Virginia Law Review*, to which Llewellyn contributed a paper. There was a broad consensus in favor of the bill before Congress, but a number of detailed criticisms were voiced. Concurrently the Rome Institute for Unification of Private Law had been actively concerned with preparation of a Uniform Law on International Sale of Goods with which Llewellyn had been briefly associated in 1931–2. A second draft of this was published in 1939...Naturally all of these activities were followed closely by Llewellyn. For nearly twenty years he had specialized in this area and he had for a long time been highly critical of the Uniform Sales Act. [Accordingly,] Llewellyn saw a Federal Sales Act as a means of promoting general reform of the law of sales. If Congress acted, it would be difficult for the states not to fall into line. On the other hand, a majority of the Executive Committee of the NCCUSL, including the President, William A. Schnader, saw a Federal Sales Act which diverged from the Uniform Sales Act as a serious threat to uniformity. Furthermore, Schnader himself was a supporter of decentralized government and was suspicious of moves which might increase the influence of Congress over commercial law. In October 1937 the NCCUSL rejected a motion by Llewellyn that a committee should be set up to follow and cooperate with the preparation of a federal sales bill. Instead, it resolved that the Federal Sales Act should conform as nearly as possible with the Uniform Sales Act. However, there was a good deal of sympathy with Llewellyn's ideas. At the same meeting it was decided to invite him to take over the chairmanship of the Commercial Acts section and Schnader indicated that it was still open to him to pursue plans for reform of the Uniform Sales Act and that the defeat of his motion should not be treated as a matter of consequence.

In the long term the delay in the enactment of the Federal Sales Bill and the initial caution of the NCCUSL were a blessing for Llewellyn. For after 1939 the initiative for pursuing the matter passed to the NCCUSL and during the next stage, the preparation of a Revised Uniform Sales Act came to be treated as a pilot project for a much more ambitious matter, a comprehensive commercial code. It was Schnader who was responsible for the transition. He had become

President of the NCCUSL after a period of relative inactivity by that body. He was one of a reform-minded group in the organization who were anxious to make it more effectual. The record of the NCCUSL up to that time showed that the one area in which there had been a relatively consistent demand for uniformity had been commercial law. In September 1940, at the 50th Annual Meeting of the NCCUSL in Philadelphia, Schnader in his Presidential Address took the opportunity to review generally the work of the conference and to put forward some ideas for the future activities. The first public suggestion for a comprehensive code was introduced briefly, almost casually, in this speech:

> Our splendid commercial acts were prepared and adopted by this Conference many years ago. Many changes in methods of transacting business have taken place in the meanwhile. In addition, they were adopted and recommended piecemeal. In a number of respects, there is overlapping and duplication, and in some instances, inconsistency, in dealing wih negotiable instruments, bills of lading, warehouse receipts, stock transfers, sales and trust receipts. Could not a great uniform commercial code be prepared, which would bring the commercial law up to date, and which could become the uniform law of our fifty-three jurisdictions, by the passage of only fifty-three acts, instead of many times that number?

This statement marks the beginning of a public campaign for a Code, but it had been anticipated by a great deal of preparatory work. Three memoranda by Llewellyn on plans for the Code survive in his papers, all dated 1940 and preceding Schnader's speech to the conference. They do not tell the whole story, but they clearly indicate that Llewellyn and Schnader were working closely together and were the two people most active in developing the idea at this stage. The original idea may have been Schnader's but nearly all of the first detailed planning was done by Llewellyn. By the time of the first official announcement the general strategy in respect of objectives, scope and method had been worked out. Although this strategy changed over time, the basic conceptions survived for the most part and they represent some of the most important and visible aspects of Llewellyn's contribution.

Discussion Question: Twining says that the Code was packaged as state law instead of federal law in part because some of the sponsors feared the possibility of an invasive centralized government that controlled too many aspects of people's lives. Does this fear still make sense today? Given the widening scope of federal regulation over our lives, do you see any problem with allowing federal law to govern commercial transactions?

Taking Commercial Law Seriously
Dennis Patterson[3]

The Uniform Commercial Code (the "Code") is the singular expression of a jurisprudential vision. As the conventional wisdom suggests, American Legal Realism was both a reaction to Legal Formalism as well as a striking vision of the role of law in modern society. The Code was, of course, fashioned in the image of one of its principal architects, Karl N. Llewellyn. No jurisprudence of the Code is possible without some account of Llewellyn's jurisprudence and the "realism" he fostered in his great legislative achievement.

Formalism, at least Langdellian formalism [Langdell was a professor at Harvard Law School in the late nineteenth century], was a vision of law in the manner of early modernist science. Like the natural scientists he so admired, Langdell wanted to uncover the logic of law, a logic that he believed was hidden beneath the play of judicial decision-making. As he famously said,

> Law, considered as a science, consists of certain principles or doctrines. To have such a mastery of these as to be able to apply them with constant facility and certainty to the evertangled skein of human affairs, is what constitutes a true lawyer; and hence to acquire that mastery should be the business of every earnest student of law. Each of these doctrines has arrived at its present state by slow degrees; in other words, it is a growth, extending in many cases through centuries. This growth is to be traced in the main

3. Dennis Patterson, Taking Commercial Law Seriously: From Jurisprudence to Pedagogy, 74 Chi.-Kent L. Rev. 625 (1999). Copyright 1999 by Illinois Institute of Technology. Reprinted by permission; Dennis Patterson, Good Faith, Lender Liability, and Discretionary Acceleration: Of Llewellyn, Wittgenstein, and the Uniform Commercial Code, 68 Tex. L. Rev. 169 (1989). Copyright 1989 by the Texas Law Review Association. Reprinted by permission.

through a series of cases; and much the shortest and best, if
not the only way of mastering the doctrine effectually is by
studying the cases in which it is embodied. But the cases
which are useful and necessary for this purpose at the present day bear an exceedingly small proportion to all those
that have been reported. The vast majority are useless and
worse than useless for any purpose of systematic study.
Moreover, the number of fundamental legal doctrines is
much less than is commonly supposed; the many different
guises in which the same doctrine is constantly making its
appearance, and the great extent to which legal treatises
are a repetition of each other, being the cause of much misapprehension. If these doctrines could be so classified and
arranged that each should be found in its proper place, and
nowhere else, they would cease to be formidable from their
number.

To be sure, Llewellyn's realism was a rejection of Langdellian formalism. But it is important to appreciate that, like Langdell, Llewellyn
did not reject the idea that law could be found. Rather, Llewellyn
thought that the law Langdell found hidden was already in plain
view. Unlike Langdell, who believed that the state of the law could be
divine from underlying principles, Llewellyn rejected the idea that
rules or principles were the best source for divining the law of a
transaction. For this, one must turn to commercial practices.

There is no better confirmation of this characterization than the
text of the Code itself. Consider the definition of "Agreement" in 1-
201(3):

"Agreement" means the bargain of the parties in fact as
found in their language or by implication from other circumstances including course of dealing or usage of trade or
course of performance as provided in this Act (Sections 1-
205 and 2-208). Whether an agreement has legal consequences is determined by the provisions of this Act, if applicable; otherwise by the law of contracts (Section 1-103).

When asking whether the parties have an Agreement, and what the
content of that Agreement might be, one looks not to legal norms but
to what the Code refers to (without definition) as "the bargain of the
parties in fact." The task of a judge is not to look at the facts and
couple those with norms to reach a legal conclusion. Rather, the

judge is to look at the facts as they would be viewed by a similarly-situated merchant and, on that basis, draw a conclusion.

The Realist vision of law is profoundly different from formalism and, yet, strangely similar. The Realist—in this case, Llewellyn—is not denying that "law" has a source, rather, he is just locating the source in a different place...

Llewellyn's vision closely resembles the hermeneutic circle. To define the agreement of the parties, one must look at their language. To understand the language, one must investigate the commercial background of its use. To determine the expectations of the parties, one must evaluate both their language and the circumstances surrounding contract formation. Thus, understanding any single element requires an understanding of the totality.

Limiting the agreement of the parties to the written words alone crabs the contextual character of the Code concept of agreement. Meaning is wider than words alone. Like his contemporary, Ludwig Wittgenstein, Llewellyn recognized that meaning is a function of words in context. Wittgenstein's famous aphorism could just as easily have come from Llewellyn: "[T]he meaning of a word is its use in the language"...

[Patterson then analyzes the concept of "good faith" which is imported into every contract under the Code via 1-203, and which is supposed to prevent unfair surprise by requiring each party to behave in an honest manner in conformity with prevailing customs, thereby protecting the other party's reasonable expectations]. The intellectual history of the drafting of the Code reveals that the notion of expectation—specifically reasonable commercial expectation—provides the central component of the good faith/expectation/agreement trinity. Understandably, then, in his effort to make the law responsive to commercial practice, Llewellyn believed that participants in commercial practices should shape the development of law. Specifically, Llewellyn, in an effort to revive an earlier practice, advocated a central role for merchant juries in judging the merits of commercial disputes. To Llewellyn, the special commercial court of factfinder was essential to the orderly development and critique of commercial practices. A jury of similarly situated business persons, unlike a lay jury, was capable of judging the nuances of commercial practice.

This distrust of the nonprofessional, however, was not elitist but philosophical. Llewellyn did not see the exercise of judgment as a purely cognitive process, as it was for the classicists. Instead, judgment—the ability to subsume facts under broad legal categories—required experience grounded in practice...

Perhaps more than any other modern theorist of commercial law, Llewellyn was aware that commercial practices are inseparable from the social critique of those practices. The meaning of a practice—commercial, social, or otherwise—is not readily apparent. Like any other text, a commercial practice must be interpreted; its meaning is not self-evident from the behavior of the participants in the practice. Instead, the participants offer constructive accounts of the meaning and significance of what they do.

The Code concept of agreement expands the range of materials from which litigants can fashion arguments about the meaning of their commercial practices. When disagreement arises over the reasonableness of expectations against the background of an ongoing practice such as lending, the parties offer a factfinder narrative reconstructions of the point of the practice. In short, each side tells a story to support its claim that its expectation is, under the circumstances, reasonable. Thus, "good faith" describes behavior that protects the reasonable expectations of the parties. The factfinder evaluates reasonableness against the background of an ongoing practice whose normative nature is properly the subject of contested and competing narrative accounts. To reach a conclusion, the factfinder must determine the degree to which each alternative narrative reconstruction of the agreement is consistent with the particular social context out of which the dispute arose...Llewellyn's approach to language reflects fundamental philosophical presuppositions about the nature of social reality: that its meaning is contestable and that different persons will have different points of view on both the meaning and the significance of merchant practices. Llewellyn thus confronted a problem with which his contemporary, Wittgenstein, also grappled: the inside-outside distinction [namely, the relation between meanings embedded in social practices versus meanings in the minds of individual actors].

Wittgenstein replaced the idea of meaning in the head with the idea of meaning in activities of which persons are a part. Many of these activities are governed by rules, which are themselves the subject of interpretation. Rule following is, in fact, a practice. Disputes will, of course, arise about what constitutes following a rule. But the basic contours of disagreement will have been set, for disagreement about the application of a rule is grounded in training, which provides the foundation for agreements (and disagreements) in interpretive judgments. In arguing for one interpretation of a rule over another, participants in the practice appeal to the point of the practice as a ground for their claims to contextual meaning. Like Llewellyn, Wittgenstein filled the gap between mind and meaning "with the longstanding custom of the community." Wittgenstein believed that meaning is neither "in the mind" nor "in the word"; it is in the activity that gives life to the word. Hence, the meaning of a word is its use in the language ...

Of the two central components of Llewellyn's vision of a revised sales law, one died and one remained. The merchant-jury idea did not survive past the Second Revised Uniform Sales Act. The component that remained, Llewellyn's conception of agreement, was carried forward into the new Uniform Commercial Code. The demise of the merchant jury marked the breakdown of Llewellyn's unitary vision of commercial practice. [Under the final version of the Code,] commercial practice was to be regulated by the community at large. Transferring the function of critique to non-merchants had the inevitable effect of creating a rift between the merchant community and the larger social structure. The role of critiquing merchant practice, once an important part of the life of the merchant community, was surrendered to persons who would judge the propriety of commercial practice on an episodic basis and from an "eccentric" perspective.

The critique of commercial practices—whether of merchants, lenders, lessors, or other participants— from a position outside the contours of participants' self-understanding subjects the meaning of the practices to radical change. By expanding the sources used to determine the meaning of a practice beyond the letter of the parties' agreement, the Code inexorably expands the range and scope of critique. This function, which Llewellyn wanted to limit to merchant juries, is now the responsibility of civil juries. A civil jury's judgments of what is reasonable conduct will necessarily be different from those of a merchant jury, because members of a civil jury will base their judgments on presupposition or "prejudice" different from that of persons in the trade.

The merits of using civil juries are, of course, debatable. In any event, the failure of Llewellyn's merchant-jury proposal has materially affected the development of modern commercial law doctrine. At the level of social theory, the elimination of the merchant jury marks a point in the evolution of contract doctrine away from a Nineteenth-century individualist dogma to a more relational, communitarian, and intersubjective view of the relationship of the individual to the group. By entrusting civil juries with the tasks of constructing the meaning of the parties' agreement and of judging the reasonableness of the commercial practices out of which that meaning arises, the Code inexorably establishes that community members—not participants in commercial practices—are the arbiters of normative, communal conflict.

Discussion Question: What is your opinion of the two radical ideas that Llewellyn sought to advance through the Code, namely anti-formalism and the merchant-jury? First, does it make sense to incorporate social practices into the parties' agreement per 1-201(3), or does this render contracts too amorphous by adding terms and conditions that the parties have not explicitly approved as binding? Second, do you favor specialized juries (or specialized courts) for business disputes, a tradition dating back to Lord Mansfield, or is this anathema to the basic democratic principles underlying the use of juries in the first place?

Chapter Two

Drafting the Code and Getting it Enacted

Work on the Code began in the early 1940s, but due to the enormity of the project, the Code was not completed as a unified whole until 1951. A full text-and-comments version did not appear until 1952, just in time for the Code to be enacted in the first state, Pennsylvania, in 1953. Although the Code was only adopted by a handful of states during the 1950s, it was thereafter adopted rapidly, in large part because the Code proved its mettle in the states where it had been enacted.

The first reading in this chapter is an early commentary by Professor Braucher, tracing the drafting of the Code and the early struggle for enactment. Braucher explains that the Code was introduced to the New York legislature in 1953, but they referred it to the New York Law Revision Commission, which held hearings on the Code for several years, reviewing it with a fine-toothed comb. Many of the concerns raised by the Commission led to the subsequent amendments to the Code, resulting in a completely revised text-and-comments version of the Code in 1958.

The second selection in this chapter contains Karl Llewellyn's presentation to the New York Law Revision Committee in 1954, when he urged adoption of the Code and expressed incredulity at the resistance marshaled against the Code.

The final selection comes from Soia Metschikoff, Llewellyn's student and research assistant at Columbia University, who later became his drafting partner, and finally, wife and colleague. Metschikoff was appointed Assistant Reporter of the Code and had a strong hand in its drafting and subsequent adoption. Long after Llewellyn's death in 1962, Metschikoff played a major role in furthering the Code project. This selection contains her personal reflections on the Code project, providing an rare, informal glimpse from behind-the-scenes.

Legislative History of the Uniform Commercial Code
Robert Braucher[1]

The Code itself began with the address of President William Schnader to the 50th annual meeting of the NCCUSL (the "Conference") in 1940. The proposal had the concurrence of Professor Karl N. Llewellyn, then of Columbia Law School, chairman of the Commercial Acts Section of the Conference, and work was promptly begun on a Uniform Revised Sales Act as a major subdivision of the proposed Code. In 1942, the American Law Institute (the "Institute") agreed to participate, and the Uniform Revised Sales Action was approved by the Conference in 1943 and by the Institute in 1944. Professor Llewellyn was the reporter and Miss Soia Mentschikoff was the assistant reporter in the first part of the project; they later became chief reporter and associate chief reporter for the Code as a whole.

The comprehensive joint project officially got under way January 1, 1945. Supervision of the Code was the responsibility of a five-man editorial board, under the chairmanship of Judge Herbert F. Goodrich. The method of operation, described in the initial comment to the Code, followed in outline the Institute's procedure in work on the various Restatements. A draft prepared by one of the reporters was reviewed by a small group of "advisers," then by the Council of the Institute and by a section of the Conference. Finally, the draft approved by these bodies was submitted to the general membership of the Institute and the Conference, often at a joint meeting. By May 1949 the Code had reached the stage of an integrated draft of nine articles with notes and comments.

From the beginning the Section of Corporation, Banking and Business Law of the American Bar Association took an interest in the Code project. As the project neared completion a committee of the Section reviewed the sponsors' draft and made numerous suggestions. During the summer of 1950 the sponsors organized an enlarged editorial board, consisting of sixteen members. Early in 1951 the board held a meeting at which the ABA Section and other interested groups presented criticisms of the Code and proposals for changes. The editorial board subsequently approved a number of these proposals and

---

1. This article originally appeared at 58 Colum. L. Rev. 798 (1958), Copyright 1958 by Columbia University. Reprinted by permission.

incorporated them in the definitive text which was approved in 1951 by joint meetings of the two sponsoring organizations and by the House of Delegates of the American Bar Association.

Editorial work, drafting of comments, and printing continued for another year, supervised by Professor Charles Bunn of the University of Wisconsin. A full text and comments edition embodying the Code as finally approved was not available until 1952. In that year the Code was introduced "for educational purposes only" in the legislatures of California, Mississippi, and New York. In 1953 it was introduced in California, Connecticut, Illinois, Indiana, Massachusetts, Mississippi, New Hampshire, and Pennsylvania. During 1952 the editorial board was reactivated to consider objections and suggestions arising as the Code was introduced, and in 1952 and 1953 the board approved a number of minor amendments which were subsequently ratified by the Institute and the Conference.

As the Code neared completion, published references to it increased in volume. A judicial opinion stated that provisions of the Code "which do not conflict with statute or settle case law are entitled to as much respect and weight as courts have been inclined to give to the various Restatements. It, like the Restatements, has the stamp of approval of a large body of American scholarship." People who had participated in the drafting wrote explanatory articles in legal periodicals. Annotations were prepared in Pennsylvania and later in Massachusetts and other states. After the Code's enactment in Pennsylvania [in 1953], the Pennsylvania Bankers Association published a manual on the Code and lecture series in that state were reprinted in Pennsylvania periodicals. Later the American Law Institute published a series of monographs on the Code, and new casebooks in fields covered by the Code were spattered with Code references.

The result was that groups that had not previously taken part in the project came to examine it critically. In addition to a great volume of favorable discussion, there appeared some highly critical academic comment on particular provisions of the Code. Professor Beutel of the University of Nebraska announced his all-out hostility, branding the Code as "the Lawyers and Bankers Relief Act," involving "a deliberate sell-out of the ALI and the NCCUSL to the bank lobby." The other principal opponent, Emmett F. Smith, house counsel to the Chase National Bank of New York, was in strange contrast. Late in

1952 he began a one-man campaign to defeat the Code, circulating far and wide over the nation two mimeographed memoranda of forty-odd pages each. Far more effective than the Beutel attacks, the Smith memoranda provoked a printed reply from the Conference. Opposition by other groups seems to be traceable at least in part to the Smith memorandum, and it seems a fair guess that Smith was largely responsible for the fact that no state except Pennsylvania enacted the Code before 1957.

During 1953 the Massachusetts legislature referred the Code to a recess commission and the New York legislature referred it to the New York Law Revision Commission. Early in 1954 the Massachusetts commission, by a vote of six to three, recommended enactment; a minority called for further study and for exploration of the possibility of enactment by interstate compact. Later in 1954 the Pennsylvania State Chamber of Commerce appointed a committee to study the Code, and the executive board of that Chamber adopted a favorable resolution recommending amendments. Meanwhile the New York Commission suspended all other work, appointed some twenty consultants to study the Code, and held a series of public hearings.

In view of those developments the editorial board was reactivated. During 1954 it appointed subcommittees for each of the several articles of the Code. The subcommittees reviewed all available comments and criticisms and recommended changes to text and comments to meet those criticisms thought to have merit. The editorial board reviewed these recommendations and in January 1955 published Supplement No. 1, proposing certain changes and answering criticisms which had been rejected. Bills embodying these changes were introduced, but not enacted, in the 1955 legislative sessions in Pennsylvania and Massachusetts.

During 1955 the study of the New York Commission went forward, and the subcommittees of the editorial board followed their work closely. The Commission took the view that it could report only to the legislature, but it furnished to the subcommittees the critical comments of its consultants and committees. The subcommittees reviewed the numerous problems raised and formulated tentative recommendations, making their reports available to the commission. Finally, after three years of work and the expenditure of some $300,000, the commission early in 1956 rendered its report. The report's major conclusions may be summarized as follows:

(1) The "preponderance" of the arguments for or against codification "is in favor of careful and foresighted codification of all or major parts of commercial law";

(2) Such a commercial code "would be of greater value to the public and the legal profession than the enactment, even with revisions, of separate uniform laws";

(3) Such a code "is attainable with a reasonable amount of effort and within a reasonable amount of time";

(4) The Uniform Commercial Code "is not satisfactory in its present form"; and

(5) The Uniform Commercial Code "cannot be made satisfactory without comprehensive re-examination and revision in light of all critical comment obtainable."

Following publication of the New York report, the subcommittees of the editorial board reviewed their tentative recommendations previously formulated and made final reports to the editorial board. The sponsoring organizations [the NCCUSL and the ALI] authorized the publication of a revised edition of the Code, and by November 1956 the board had completed action on a revised statutory text. That text was published early in 1957 in two volumes. One showed the language deleted from the 1952 text in square brackets and new language in italics; the other incorporated the changes in clean text. The subcommittees also prepared revised official comments during the spring of 1957, but publication was withheld to await development in the 1957 legislative sessions in Massachusetts and Pennsylvania. A complete revised text and comments edition was finally published early in 1958.

The revised text of the Code was introduced in the 1957 sessions of the legislatures in Massachusetts and Pennsylvania. It was enacted in Massachusetts in 1957 and in Kentucky in 1958. Elsewhere there seemed to be no prospect of enactment before 1959...

The use of the legislative history of the Code to help understand its provisions can best be illustrated by bringing that history to bear on specific problems. To that end the history of a few Code provisions which have troubled draftsmen, critics and revisors is given below, with references to some of the relevant literature. The illustrations are drawn primarily from Article I—General Provisions, and thus relate to the interpretation of the Code as a whole rather than to particular aspects of the law of sales, bills and notes, of chattel security.

Variation by Agreement

Section 1-102(3) now "states affirmatively at the outset that freedom of contract is a principle of the Code." It was not always so. In the 1950 version, rules enunciated by the Code were mandatory and were not to be waived or modified by agreement unless the rule was qualified by the words "unless otherwise agreed" or similar language. Professor Beutel said that "for sheer presumptuousness and impossibility of administration" that provision "takes all the prizes." Other critics made lists of sections to which the words "unless otherwise noted" should be inserted, and the ABA Section made the reversal of the presumption that all rules were mandatory one of the principal items on its agenda.

The result was that later drafts prohibited variation by agreement only with respect to definitions and formal requirements, rights and duties of third parties, and "general obligations such as good faith, due diligence, commercial reasonableness and reasonable care." Absence of the words "unless otherwise agreed" was to contain no negative implication; and except as specifically provided, variation by agreement was permissible. These provisions in turn were repeatedly criticized at the New York hearings, and a revision was proposed by the editorial board. The New York commission subsequently objected to several aspects of this revised provision.

The 1957 text meets all the points made by the commission but one. Freedom of contract is stated affirmatively at the outset, subject only to specific exceptions and a general exception for "the obligations of good faith, diligence, reasonableness and care prescribed by this Act." On the recommendation of the commission, the exceptions to definitions and formal requirements and for rights and duties of third parties were deleted as unnecessary. The exception for "general obligations" is limited to four listed types of obligation. As in earlier versions, "the parties may by agreement determine the standards by which performance of such obligations is to be measured if such standards are not manifestly unreasonable."

The point urged by the New York commission but not accepted by the sponsors was that "a general prohibition of disclaimer of obligations of diligence, reasonableness and care is unsound." It is not clear whether the commission was criticizing policy or merely drafting technique; more specific prohibitions of disclaimer contained in other sections were noted without disapproval. There was a clear difference of opinion, however, as to section 4-403 which provides that a customer may order his bank to stop payment of an item if he gives the bank a reasonable opportunity to act on the order. The comment makes it clear that in cases of mistaken payment in violation of such an order section 4-103(1) is to apply, thus denying effect to an agreement disclaiming the bank's responsibility for failure to exercise ordinary care. The result would be to change New York law and adopt the rule established by judicial decision in many states. The New York commission asserted that in New York liability in such cases "is not for failure of ordinary care but merely upon its debt to its customer, and despite the contrary assumption in comments to Section 4-403, nothing in Article 4 would change this rule or make Section 4-103(1) applicable." The editorial board disagreed as to the proper interpretation of the Code, and stood firm on both drafting and policy.

Use of Comments

The uniform acts promulgated by the Conference have from the beginning been accompanied by brief commissions' notes. The original Uniform Sales Act was given more elaborate exposition in the treatise of the draftsman. The treatise has been taken as stating the legislative intent even though it was first published three years after the Act was promulgated. Early in the Code project that precedent was referred to as an anomaly involving the "delegation to private persons of essentially legislative power." As a substitute, it was proposed that official comments should be prepared to make clear what changes were made in the law and why, and that the Code should expressly refer to the comments as a guide to its construction and application.

Perhaps inevitably, the comments seemed to many to be less accurate than the text, and the question was raised repeatedly whether specific reference to the comments in the statutory text was sound legislative practice. At the suggestion of the ABA Section, provisions were added to Section 1-102(3) in 1951 that "if text and comment conflict, text controls" and that "prior drafts of text and comments may not be used to ascertain legislative intent." Revision of a number of comments was recommended in Supplement No. 1, and the revised comments published in 1958 included many corrections as well as changes required by text amendments. The New York commission believed that the direct invitation to consult the comments was "unnecessary and could lead to unprecedented use of the Comments to expand and qualify the text."

The editorial board in the 1956 revision deleted from the Code text all reference to the comments. That decision did not rest on the fears expressed by the New York commission and others. In practice the courts of Pennsylvania had accepted the Code's invitation to consult the comments, and there was no indication of any unsound result. But in 1956 the 1952 comments "were clearly out of date and it was know when any new ones could be prepared;" moreover, "the changes from the text enacted in Pennsylvania in 1953 are clearly legitimate legislative history." By the time a bill was prepared in 1957 for introduction in Indiana, new comments were in process, and the Indiana bill restored the provisions as to comments. To the prohibition on use of prior drafts, the Indiana bill added a prohibition on the use of "analyses, testimony, reports or articles respecting such prior drafts" ...

[Note to Readers: The details are not so important at this juncture: Braucher is merely pointing out that the Code has changed its position with respect to whether its terms can be varied by agreement, and whether the text of the Code should make reference to the comments. He is also raising the question about what constitutes legitimate 'legislative history' of the Code, e.g., whether a party can support its position by referring to prior versions of the Code, or whether the changes that were made to the Code should not count as legislative history in the traditional sense because they were not made by a legislature. The operative question is whether courts should have recourse to prior drafts of the Code to adduce conclusions about why the Code is presently structured as it is.]

It is the belief of the sponsors that for most purposes examination of prior drafts and analysis of controversies now laid to rest will add little light to that shed by the official comments. The author's own view is that resort to legislative history will be helpful only in unusual cases. The reader may decide for himself, however, whether it would be wise, in the manner of the 1957 Indiana bill, to enjoin judges from reading such an article as this.

Discussion Question: This article raises an interesting question about the materials that a court should consult in construing the Code. Obviously, a court can look to the text of the Code itself, and then to the comments, but the picture gets murkier if the court wants to go deeper into the history of a provision. Since the Code is a model statute that was not introduced and debated by the legislatures in most states, the 'legislative history' of the Code is virtually non-existent in many states. Generally, examining the 'legislative history' of the Code involves looking at prior drafts of a section, along with any comments from the New York Law Revision Commission, as well as law review articles discussing earlier versions of the Code. If you were handling a Code case, how might you use 'legislative history' to support your reading of a provision?

Statement to The New York Law Revision Commission
Karl N. Llewellyn[2]

SOME REASONS FOR ADOPTING THE UNIFORM COMMERCIAL CODE

A. *Because of Who Backs the Code*

In the entire discussion of the Uniform Commercial Code not one person has appeared (outside of Louisiana) who has not applauded the Uniform Commercial Acts as being at least each in its own day a sound job, a wise job, and a useful job. These Uniform Commercial Acts were prepared for the country by the National Conference of Commissioners on Uniform State Laws. They were prepared one by one, in the period ranging from 1895 through 1934. These Acts include the Negotiable Instruments Law, the Uniform Sales Act, the Uniform Warehouse Receipts Act (in partnership with the Warehousemen's Association), the Uniform Bills of Lading Act, the Uniform Stock Transfer Act, the Uniform Trust Receipts Act. The National Conference of Commissioners—the members are officials appointed by the several States to prepare uniform laws—has also spent many sessions in work over piecemeal amendments, in sustained efforts to modernize the old Acts without changing their framework; and it has spent many, many sessions on problems of chattel security and of bank collection.

This is the body, with this now sixty-year record of careful work, with this record of unchallenged success whenever its product has

---

2. From William Twining, Karl Llewellyn and the Realist Movement (Norman: University of Oklahoma Press, 1973). Reprinted by permission.

been put to the test of being *enacted law at work*—that is the body which has prepared and which now stands behind the Uniform Commercial Code—a Code over which the Conference, beginning in 1940, worked for more than ten years before the appearance of even a first tentative final draft. What reason can there be for believing that this great law-preparing body has so changed its nature as to have lost either the competence or the wisdom demonstrated by its record? No single person, since discussion of the Code began, has suggested any reason for thinking that the skill which built the old Acts is not with us still, in modern form. No man has dared to!

This is the Conference which backs the Code with knowledge of it, and after years of labor over it and with it, and with enthusiasm.

The Conference of Commissioners on Uniform State Laws is not alone in this. A partnership was formed in 1943 between that Conference and the leading productive law-organization of these United States, the American Law Institute, the organization which had produced, by its own slow, sure and carefully tested methods, the famed Restatement of the Law. The Institute had previously left out of its labors the whole field of commercial law, as being a field already occupied, magnificently occupied, by the Conference.

In 1943 the two organizations put into partnership, in order to produce the Uniform Commercial Code, their resources, their slowly built-up know-how, their manpower [Note to Readers: A formal agreement between the NCCUSL and the ALI was reached in 1944 to pursue the Code as a joint project]. The American Law Institute also backs the Uniform Commercial Code. It also does so after years of labor with and over that Code.

B. *Because of How the Code was Built*

Article by Article there was one draftsman, or a team of two, preparing, presenting, revising. The drafter's work was under steady criticism and revision, typically in three-day sessions every six to ten weeks by a group of advisors which included experts in the field of law concerned, experts in the field of business or finance concerned, and also lawyers or judges of general experience and no expertness whose important business was to see that it all made sense and that each part could be understood by men who were not experts. Results of any meeting were worked over, tested out, and brought in again for any misguess to be gone over afresh. There was constant correspondence and consultation with any outside experts in the business or law concerned who could be discovered and who would give the time. At all times the central planning and drafting staff were in on the drafting; in also on the discussions, to keep continuity, to add their own experience and expertness, and to keep the gears of the whole Code meshed; in on the presentations, to assure any group or floor that this was not only a whole-job but a whole-team job.

Each year's work (sometimes each half-year's) came for review in two- to four-day sessions before each of two singularly able general reviewing bodies; the Commercial Acts (or Property Acts) Section of the Conference, each a group of 11 notable for its experienced down-to-earth practicing lawyer's approach to the text of any proposed law, and the Council of the Institute, a group of 30 notable especially for the membership of a large number of able judges who size up any proposed law as a court would. Only as the text of the year's work was shaped up by these bodies did it come to the floors of the organizations.

Floor discussion was again in detail, section by section, with the sustained attention of experienced lawyers from every section of the country, always including men who had represented various diverse interests, men of long experience in the details concerned, plus a most valuable range of men who had one such case, or two or three (in the net an astounding range of experience), with many men also directing their attention in one large part to whether the text made general sense, and could be easily read. At this point let two further things be said: (a) The floor *worked,* in these sessions, over all the years. They gave attention, they followed text and debate, they did solid thinking. (b) Few votes, in any early stage, were 'binding,' save where the underlying plan of some piece of the work had to be determined. 'Suggestions' or 'recommendation for study' was the type of action. The work of one year's floor was thus as a *standard practice reviewed the next year,* after testing in between the staff, by the advisors, by the Sections of the Conference, by the Council of the Institute.

As the work moved toward completion, it came further under the due attention and fire of critics of all kinds: experts from the law schools, representative committees of interested industries or other groups, bar association committees, concerned peculiarly with the effect on the law of their particular State, and the like. All suggestions were worked over, often in detailed discussions which led to solutions of increased value and to satisfaction to all concerned.

This process of critique, and occasionally of real improvement in minor detail, has gone on even after the Code had come into seemingly final form.

Two things are notable about it: (1) The criticisms which have been proved to have bite have touched a very small portion of the Code indeed. In regard to any single area of the present law, the clear improvements made by the Code outnumber and outweigh between twentyfold and a hundredfold such minor errors as have been brought to light by even certain bitter chasers after error. And each real error or even semi-error which had been turned up *has been duly cured*. (2) The men who have tested the Code in use and for use, by running it against the problems of a law course or against the problems of a daily practice: these men have become vigorous proponents of the Code. The men who have studied it carefully have found their study turning them into enthusiasts. Doubts vanish like haze on a summer morning.

The type of use-testing just referred to builds a foundation of peculiar confidence. Because a kit of tools, whether of rules of law or of anything else, if it is either ill-designed or ill-chosen turns up not only an occasional bug on the things in mind, but also an antheap of bugs on any job not consciously planned for. Whereas a well-designed and well-chosen kit of tools will handle in unplanned comfort any number of unforeseen jobs which may turn up.

The Code has proven, in *sharp contrast to the existing law,* to be a good and well-designed kit of legal tools.

In sum: a more carefully and fully tested piece of legislation has never been presented in these United States.

C. *Because of Why it was Necessary to Build the Code*

For a free economy, for soundly developing American enterprise and competition, it is of the essence that the rules of the game should be as simple as possible, and that those rules of the game should be readily known to all.

The first and best reason for the Code is that the law which governs our commerce and commercial finance is substantially unknown to most lawyers, whether they need to know it or not, and is almost wholly unknown to most business men.

The business men do not know even when they need to consult a lawyer. One major job which the old Uniform Commercial Acts did do was to cut down, so far as they went, the unknown character of the law by reducing parts of it to relatively clear language, easy to find. And that was both good and even then badly needed. It showed the way.

But first, those Acts covered much less than half of the most needed ground; and next their text has now come to be overlaid by a mass of case-law which is almost as difficulty work through as was the law before those Acts; and again, new conditions have opened up new problems which in turn present new areas of unknown (or non-existent and therefore unknowable) law.

Law unknown is law which is uncomfortable, and which is expensive, and which is uncertain—and, which is indeed unfair. Important general areas of law have no business to be the monopoly of a relatively few experts, serving a relatively few clients. Business and finance are matters vital to all American enterprise, be that enterprise large or small, be it rural or metropolitan; sound, clear, legal advice at a reasonable rate is good for American business and finance: how else is competition to be fair and free? Such advise reduces risks, it reduces disputes, it makes for quick and fair adjustment.

Such advice, necessary to a free-running economy, cannot but be bad when the law is unknown or is hard to uncover or is confused when found. That difficulty the Code cures to a degree and on a scale hitherto almost unmatched in American law...

The actual historical reasons for undertaking the Code have their own further and independent powerful punch.

(a) Much of the law, whether embodied in the original Uniform Commercial Acts or not, has become outmoded as the nature of business, of technology, and of financing has changed. Such law needs to be brought up to date.

(b) Akin to this is the continuing presence in the law of a large number of technical traps which can—in an era of bad times or in a situation of bad feeling—be used in bad faith to do outrage. These need cure.

(c) Both in areas of growth outside the old Uniform Acts and in wide troubling areas within them there is much case-law which is in conflict as between States and in confusion even within a State. These matters need to be cleared up.

(d) The existing law presents two lines of problems which involve one most needed quality: to wit, the best that we can do in regard to making law simple...

All of the above calls for re-examination and revision of commercial rules of law. But why in the form of a Code? In the first place, experience has shown wide and unhappy gaps to exist between the existing Acts. Secondly, prior work over any type of reform has turned up repeated problems which leaped across the 'boundaries' of the traditional 'fields' of law...

D. *Because of How Much the Code Brings into Clear Form, Easy to Find*

If all that the Uniform Commercial Code has done had been to bring together, sort out, modernize and harmonize the old Uniform Commercial Code Acts, together with a Bulk Sales Act and a new and uniform version of the old laws on accounts receivable, and the like—if that had been all the Code did, it still would be a tremendously worthwhile job...

But the Code does much more. The Code does not merely bring to suppliers from all over the nation *one* Bulk Sales Law instead of who-knows-how-many; it brings, in Article 6, the best which long experience has suggested [Note to Readers: Article 6 has been repealed in most states at the behest of the NCCUSL and the ALI]. The Code does not merely make sure that a decision about transfer of a bill of lading will be indexed so that persons interested in transfer of warehouse receipts can find the decision—the Code also clears up doubts which have proved troublesome and provides (as with realization in case of mercantile storage) streamlined procedures which do the job better than the present law.

And the Code really *covers* the commercial field in a way in which no present statute does. It is so queer to find no single one of the Code's opponents mentioning this fact. Where the present law is blank or else confused or else in conflict, the Code moves in, with competence based on net experience, to provide one single and very reasonable answer, which is so much more clear than the existing law that if a counselor or business man really knew how unclear the existing law is *in the case of pinch*, he ought to be hailing the Code, again, for this cause alone. For it is true that even bad rules can be worked with (though unhappily) if they are rules clear to everyone, and if they are rules known or knowable to all. On rules clearly known, a soundly free-running American economy depends. The Uniform Commercial Code provides such rules.

If you have any trouble, ask yourself or your client or your lawyer any one of the following questions which any one can match by the hundred.

(a) You receive a 'check' 'payable through' another bank: can you become a holder in due course?

(b) You invite bids, for the known purpose of preparing your own bid, and you get a 'firm' sub-bid. Can you rely on it?

(c) You have what you think to be all the necessary papers, but the transfer agent wants more, and you are pressed for time. Can you force registration of transfer?

This is the kind of unnoticed thing which the Code *covers,* in one detail after another upon another, *for the effective guidance of any lawyer or businessman, or financier*. The existing law does not...

Meantime there is, here in the Uniform Commercial Code the heaping up, the bulking up, the towering up, in those hardly countable, those hardly observable, filing details which the Code— *without any mentioning even suggesting any single detail*—proceeds to provide as seashells are provided on a seashore.

What do I do, *in any pitch,* if the bill or note is maybe not 'negotiable?' (About three hundred scattered and unfindable cases handled clearly in one section.)

What do I do, *in any pinch,* when the draft carries a 'referee in case of need?' (You find a case!)

What am I to do, *in any pinch,* with a check which comes in among a hundred—or thousand—check batch, but is indorsed by my correspondent's depositor "for acct," if I begin to worry about my correspondent, which carries its account with me?

Or: to shift to the more commercial end: If my delivery is off by a hair, can he, *in any pinch,* reject it?

Or: If I am a buyer: You mean I should pay a ten percent advance, and then when I reject good goods I get a lien, and then I can keep them out from his re-inspection and resell them to make evidence of deficiency, and then....?? You mean...?

Under the present law, such things raise doubts or dangers. Under existing law, they are tough. Under existing law, they are either wide open or plain, trouble, each, and all, and many more.

The Uniform Commercial Code cuts down the doubts, and cuts them down wisely, on literally hundreds of such things. The friends of the Code have come to take that for granted. They hardly mention it...

E. *Because of the Nature of the Code Material*

As compared with the existing law in New York or any other state:

(1) What the Code says is relatively clear. The existing law is doubtful or empty throughout almost the whole area discussed by the Code's opponents.

(2) What the Code says fits with modern business and finance. Where it changes existing law, the existing law will stand—if it gets appealed to, as it does in bad times—in the way of sense, and some honest operator will get stuck.

(3) What the Code says makes for fairness. Where it changes existing law it is where the existing law, as so often, makes trouble or sets traps for people who are acting in business good faith.

(4) What the Code says makes it relatively easy to set up transactions with fairness and with safety. Under the existing law this is a hard job, and unless a business or financing man happen by accident to draw an ace of counsel or he cuts the legal deck, the business man runs unnecessary risk or he incurs unnecessary expense or both.

(5) What the Code says leads to relative simplicity plus safety, in action. No informed person can fairly claim any such thing for the existing law of New York or of any other State.

In sum: The Code makes business and financing sense. The existing law makes neither, and is sought to be avoided by the commercial community by drafting (never wholly trustworthy, always expensive) and by arbitration (never wholly trustworthy, and in times of real hardship, a bending reed to lean on).

F. *The Code, although both large and new, is unbelievably easy to use*

Never, in American history has any statute, much less a large one such as the Code, been presented to bench, bar and public in form *so easy* and *so safe* for any man to use.

Accompanying the Code statutory sections are comments—the use of which is explicitly authorized by the Code itself—comments which give useful indication of the purpose of the section, and which do more: they cross-refer to almost everything else in the Code which bears upon the section in hand; they give clear cross-reference to the definition of any word of art whatever which the section may contain. To this add a thing: the captions of the sections have been worked over for years in order to make sure that they contain catch-words which will index all of the substance of any section.

If that were all, it would be enough to make use of this new Code easier than use of any ordinary, short, and simple statute. But that is not all...

G. *Because the gains from the Code outweigh even uniformity*

Suppose some other State, or thirty-seven other States, get chased into non-adoption of the Uniform Commercial Code. *It still is worth adoption* by any State large or small, 'commercial' or 'non-commercial.'

The proof of that has lain, now these ten years, in the law school classroom.

Present the Code to your class, and because it makes rather simple sense, they get it with three to four times the speed with which they 'get' the 'ordinary' law of any of the subject matter. With that background, they then proceed with equal speed to 'get' the ordinary law, in supplement and in comparison.

No lawyer in a Code State will ever have difficulty dealing with, or indeed in outmaneuvering, his intellectual equal from an old-fashioned State. The Code State lawyer is—even in cross-State transactions—on the inside, looking out. He can hit, in quiet confidence, from an understanding which only about eighteen present experts in these United States can match.

At home, meanwhile, he has simpler, more workable, and fairer law.

Such is a preliminary case for the Uniform Commercial Code

Karl N. Llewellyn,
August 16, 1954.

Discussion Question: Llewellyn gives seven reasons why the Code is superior to the then-prevailing approach, which was a patchwork of different uniform laws sitting atop a mountain of inconsistent case decisions. Does he make a convincing case—How many of the seven reasons do you find compelling?

Reflections of a Drafter
Soia Mentschikoff[3]

The Code was started when Bill Schnader first spoke to Karl Llewellyn about a uniform code. Bill Schnader was the Attorney General of the State of Pennsylvania and the Commissioner on Uniform State Laws, and at the meeting of the Commissioners on Uniform State Laws went to Karl, who was a commissioner from New York and chairman of the Commercial Act Section.

Bill Schnader said to Karl, "Would it be possible, instead of asking for piecemeal amendment or piecemeal enactment of amended statutes, to put them all together into something that would be coherent and that could be known as the Uniform Commercial Code so that we could make all of the changes with one act of the legislature?"

And Karl, of course, never being particularly humble about these things, said, "No problem at all. I'll draw you up a little outline of what it would look like."

On the basis of Karl's statement, Schnader got up at the Conference of Commissioners meeting and as his presidential address called for a Uniform Commercial Code to replace all of the commercial acts that the conference had drafted thus far.

At that time the Commercial Act Section was working particularly on several acts: a proposed Uniform Bank Collection Code, which

---

3. Soia Metschikoff, Reflections of a Drafter, originally published in 43 Ohio St. L. J. 537 (1982). Reprinted by permission.

was to replace the American Bankers Association Bank Collection Code that was the one being adopted all over the place, and a Uniform Revised Sales Act. In 1941, because the Code was in the offing, the Commissioners had before them the 1941 version of the Uniform Revised Sales Act, and that was my first accidental involvement in this process.

I was practicing downtown and I had left one firm, become general counsel of a company, which was making mannequins, and I was in, if you would believe it, the fashion industry. It was great fun, but we needed steel arm locks and wrist locks and things like that, and somehow it being 1941 the Government didn't think that that was prime use for steel. Why they had this horrible thought we didn't know, but the company was about to dissolve itself.

So in 1941 I drifted over to Columbia just as Karl was finishing a draft to take to the 1941 meeting of the Commissioners. Because we worked on the warranty article and I had been his research assistant four or five years before, he said, "I don't have time. Why don't you do these warranty points?"

And I said, "Well, how much time we got?"

He said, "We got about three days."

So he sat down, redid the warranty pieces, redid my draft, then he went happily off to wherever it was the conference met. When he came back he said, "Well, it was great. We had a fine time, everybody discussed it." He said, "There's one thing I want to ask you. It looks as though the American Law Institute may get interested in this and that there may be some money for the drafting and completion of the Uniform Revised Sales Act, and if there is, would you be willing to come and work on it?"

And I said, "Why sure, but I'm going downtown to work with the firm first," which I did.

Well, to my total surprise in about October or November of 1942, he called up and he said, "Hey, guess what? I got the money."

I said, "Money for what?" His proposal had slipped my mind at that point.

And he explained, "We've got to go to work, because we're going to put it through in 1943." And he said, "We have to do this, because it's going to be very important for the future."

So I went to my firm and said I wanted four months' leave of absence, because obviously you could do a Uniform Revised Sales Act in four months max.

Anyway, they gave it to me after much screaming and yelling and horsing around, and I worked on it from January until May, and we had a Uniform Revised Sales Act. This was a joint project with the American Law Institute.

Now, I want to stop right here to tell you one of the most important and significant things in the history of the Code. This was the format which was used in the drafting of that Act. There were three representatives from the Conference and three from the Institute, who served as an advisory committee. There was Uncle Billy Lewis, who was responsible for the first round of Restatements and was still director of the Institute, who acted as director for this project and chaired the meetings. The drafts would be prepared by Karl and me. I was then an assistant reporter on the sales article and we had a couple of research assistants who were working on it. The drafts would be gone over with the advisors. Now, I want to tell you who the advisors were because they were an interesting group.

From the Institute, for the purpose of controlling this possible madman who was going to do this whole project, was Judge Thomas Swan of the Second Circuit, who had been dean of the Yale Law School where Karl had been a student and then an early-type professor there. There was Professor Arthur Corbin whom Karl adored and called his "father in the law."

And then there was Hiram Thomas, who had been chairman of the Merchants' Association of New York Law Committee for 25 years, and who knew everything. He ran an index of his own on sales cases which was different from West's or anybody else's, because he did it for the practical import of the cases.

On the Conference side there was Charles Hardin from Newark, New Jersey, who represented banks, did some secured financing for banks, and generally operated in the banking area. There was Sterry Waterman, who at that point was just a lawyer up in Vermont involved in the dairy and milk industry and was horsing around with Washington trying to get greater subsidies for milk. But he was thoroughly aware of how the Code was developing. This is the same Sterry Waterman that later became a judge in the United States Court of Appeals for the Second Circuit. And then there was a fellow called

Willard Luther from Boston, who was a super draftsman and was a very, very bright guy. His super-draftsmanship was to eliminate all the unnecessary verbiage, and this came to be known as the "Lutherization" of the Code.

Each of these people performed a particular function of which they gradually became adept, and the functions grew by accident. It was an extraordinary group. It met for four or five days every month, and so the drafts were done over and over and over again, and we must have had any number of drafts.

Luther was magnificent, as I said, in cutting it down. Swan was very good on structure—that was his specialty. Hiram Thomas and Karl were great on policy and what was the underlying business reality. Corbin was the repository of all the case law that there ever was in contracts, and I mean that literally. There was once a discussion on the Statute of Frauds section, about which Corbin said, "I don't like this Karl."

And Corbin said, "I have read 14,000 cases, and this is not supported by the cases and it doesn't seem to make any sense in the light of the 14,000 cases that I've read."

Karl said to him, "But, Dad, have you treated the sale of goods cases as a special group?"

Corbin answered, "No, I haven't done that."

Then Karl said, "Well, if you do, this makes sense."

And Corbin said, "If you tell me that, okay, we will accept that." And they went on from there. It was that kind of confidence, that kind of care in each other, which moved the Code forward.

Now, from these groups we finally had a draft in September. By that time we were in what I might call the eighth or ninth full draft of Article 2 of the Code, then called the Uniform Revised Sales Act. That went to the Commissioners in Chicago in September of 1943.

Now, a word on the way that draft was presented to the Commissioners. First the Commercial Act Section met a week before the Conference. They went over everything inch by inch, made changes and suggestions, and did rewrites. I will never forget till the day I die— you must remember, at that point I was very young, and I was really impressed with all these old men who were sitting around working like dogs on this thing—old Judge William McLaren from Seattle,

Washington, because what we had to do at one point was to get clean copy, and in those days clean copy wasn't that easy to get. The stuff had been typed up, then we had to proof it. And all of these Commissioners, who I thought had at least ten feet in the grave, were sitting there doing the comparisons. We sat there all night comparing text.

Finally, after those of us in the Commercial Act Section made the changes, redid them, and then did the comparisons, we took them to the floor of the conference, and each section was presented, not in terms of the existing law because it was not that type of drafting. Let me hasten to add, there is no piece of this early part of the Code that was in any way drafted in terms of: "This is the existing law and it is in conflict, where shall we go?" *Never.* That is *not* the history of the Code, that is not the way it was drafted. It was drafted rather in terms of: "This is the business situation, or this is the life situation, and these are the problems. They can be resolved one way or the other. There are arguments for resolving them this way or that way. In our belief, it is better to resolve them this way." The latter approach made for intelligent discussion on the floor of what the policy should be, and whether the underlying situations were in fact the ones that we thought they were; so that from the beginning the Code had as a baseline the underlying factual life situations exposed for discussion by everybody who was present and who was involved in the process, and a very explicit statement as to why one choice was being made rather than another.

So, I went through the conference. The unconscionability section was still being drafted fifty different way because nobody was quite happy with it, including its prime draftsman; and that process continued and redrafts were made and comments began to be written. The early comments on that Act had reached a thousand pages before somebody woke up and said "This is absurd. You can't have a thousand pages of comment to an act which probably is only about 40 pages of text. It's a little peculiar. We've got to somehow cut back the comments."

Nonetheless, they were not completed when the next group met, which was when it was presented to the American Law Institute at the meeting in 1944. But it was presented first to the Council of the Institute and then to the Institute itself, with a revision in between— exactly the same way that it had been presented to the Conference of the Commissioners.

And finally, over the summer, since there had been some conflicts between the action taken by the Commissioners and some actions taken by the Institute, there was a final draft brought before the Commissioners, and at the same time, in August or September of 1944, the treaty was signed—and it was called a "treaty," not an agreement, not a pact, not a contract, it was a treaty—by two sovereign groups, the American Law Institute and the National Conference of Commissioners on Uniform State Laws. And they themselves felt they were sovereign groups. That treaty was funded by money from a foundation, which is Falk of Pittsburgh—again, Pennsylvania orientation—that had given us one hundred fifty or two hundred thousand dollars to go ahead and try to complete the Code.

The treaty was very interesting because the parties set up a small editorial board which consisted of the president of the Institute, the president of the Conference, the director of the American Law Institute, Karl, and one representative from the Institute and one from the Commissioners. The representative from the Institute was, of course, Bill Schnader. The representative from the Conference was Carl Pryor. This was the group which continued through until 1953, when an enlarged editorial board was formed. That was the Editorial Board.

Now, the thing I want you to notice is there wasn't a single expert on the editorial board; that in the drafting of the Uniform Revised Sales Act, there were no experts really involved except two of the group. But each Commissioner and each member of the Institute had something to add from his life experience and his life situation; thus the Code was never presented, never, except in terms of the exposition of what the underlying situation was as perceived by the reporters, and then going on from there as to why one solution or the other was preferable.

There were some exceptions in Article 9—some particular law that had to be cleaned up—but apart from that, it ran basically the other way.

In 1944 also there had been a young fellow out in Indiana, his name was Allison Dunham. He was busy looking up all kinds of secured transactions and preparing all kinds of memoranda and seeing whether he couldn't turn it up into blocks involving different kinds of collateral and different kinds of transactions. And all of a sudden he found he had himself a job and later he moved on to be assistant reporter and then associate reporter for Article 9.

The more immediate things that were going forward were Articles 3, 4, and 7, when Karl appointed reporters all over the place. He asked Roscoe Stefan whether he would act on 3 and 4, because Stefan had been involved in the American Bankers Association Bank Collection Code. Stefan said he couldn't: he was involved in the Antitrust Division and making money on that.

So then Karl took a step, which was viewed by many as a very dangerous step, but which he thought was a very sound step; he hired me. You must understand that I came to sales not out of a sales practice. I came to sales completely innocent, you know, like the little boy looking at the emperor's clothes and saying, "But for God's sake, he doesn't have any clothes on." All right? And that was useful; that was my great utility in the drafting of the Uniform Revised Sales Act, because if I understood it, anybody could understand it. If I could set it up in a pattern, it would be intelligible to anybody who was not an expert, and that wouldn't get it all mixed up with the experts. It would move rather in a logical way as in fact Article 2 does move, as you all know. I could do that because I wasn't hampered by any knowledge about the law to speak of. Knowledge about the law can be a great hindrance when you're trying to decide what you want to do that's sensible, as opposed to what you want to do to change the law. We never sat around asking "What are we going to do to change the law?" Because we couldn't have cared less. We wanted to do something that was sensible. If it was the same as the existing law, great; if it was different, great; it made no difference. That's the history of the Code.

As I said, the first one hired was Dunham. The second one was Prosser, and he was hired because he also was totally ignorant about negotiable instruments, and, therefore, he'd be a very good person to look anew at this; by that time the learning on negotiable instruments was voluminous—The Negotiable Instruments Law (NIL) was the oldest act. There were, I think, 89 cases of actual conflict as to what the devil the act meant, and the Banker's Bank Collection Code had further confused the situation. The other members of the Conference had tried to produce drafts and there was a certain feeling that "Well, we've got to get this on the road."

Prosser said he, too, was entitled to have an expert at his side; so he was co-opted as a part of the general drafting staff. This became a new technique because as you had reporters and associate reporters and assistant reporters for particular acts, obviously they had to meet with a central drafting staff. The central drafting staff was Karl and me, and we would meet with them apart from the advisors every three or four weeks, to see where they were going; or, if it took longer, every eight weeks. Then it would go to the advisors again, and from that point on, it would follow the same process as the Sales Act had followed, except that since the negotiable instruments articles were more complex and larger and there had been less preparation for them, they took longer. It also took longer because Prosser wanted to amend the NIL and he wouldn't sit down and rewrite it. And so it took a while to persuade him that was ridiculous. After all, he was the reporter, so you figured experience would teach him that you couldn't do it that way. Experience in fact did teach him that he couldn't do it that way, and we rewrote it.

In rewriting the law we developed a certain facility in the use of language. It was early discovered that there are 12 ways in which you could write something, but the simplest way was to say, "When thus and so and thus and so, then some legal consequence." In other words, the restatement format was really a very good statutory format and it highlighted the factual presuppositions on which everything was based.

A little later, after Prosser came in, my chum over here, Fax Leary, came in to horse around with the collections material because Prosser had gotten delayed. Prosser spent that first year or year and a half doing amendments to the NIL, and then he had the next period where he was actually working on the drafting of what became Article 3.

In the meantime, Fritz Kessler had been co-opted. He was supposed to be doing foreign remittances, traveler's checks, and letters of credit. As you know, the Code does not contain anything on foreign remittances or traveler's checks, and that's another story, as to why those two went out. But, of course, it does contain something on letters of credit. Kessler was, I think, the assistant reporter for Article 5. That's how the thing got started.

Grant Gilmore was co-opted in about 1947 because he and this fellow Axelrod had written an article where they also had tried to divide up securities into functional areas, and so that seemed like a useful thing to do, and he joined Dunham on that.

In 1948 we discovered Kripke, and he was co-opted by the central drafting staff when it met with the Article 9 people. And in 1950–51, Pete Coogan made the mistake of writing to Karl, and he'll tell you how he got roped in as a result of that mistake.

Lou Schwartz was doing Article 7, did it very happily, then we ran into the warehouse receipts section. We had to change it into the form in which it now is; there was no change in substance.

There were a lot of changes in form but not much substance after 1949 or 1950. The only article that was not completed to anybody's satisfaction on the reportorial group by 1952, when the first vote by states took place, was Article 9. It still needed one more year of work, which it didn't get. As it turned out—at that time we thought it was a mistake to go for immediate enactment—it was not a mistake. Schnader was absolutely correct. He had the Pennsylvania legislature ready to go and they went for the Code. Governor Dewey, who was supposed to send in the Act to the New York legislature, was reached by Aldrich from the Chase [Manhattan Bank], and he sent it to the Law Revision Commission instead. It was impossible to kill the Code once it had been enacted by Pennsylvania.

The single most important decision on enactment was made by Bill Schnader, when he refused to wait another year and went to Pennsylvania with the 1952 Act, and it was a decision which only Bill and Karl thought was correct. Homer Kripke thought it was wrong. I thought it was wrong, and I think Al and Grant thought it was wrong. Schnader was right. And that's how the Code came to be.

Discussion Question: This account of the drafting project reveals that a great deal of the project was doled out by Llewellyn to friends and acquaintances, or to people who happened to show up at the right place and time (e.g., the author was Llewellyn's research assistant, then girlfriend, then wife). Notice also that there were no consumer advocates involved in the drafting. Does Mentschikoff's account of the drafting process provide a humanizing element to an otherwise sterile Code, or does it reflect a more sinister closed circle of similarly-minded drafters?

Chapter Three

A Look at Karl Llewellyn

This chapter brings together three different perspectives on Karl Llewellyn, the principal architect of the Code. In the first selection, Professor David Ray Papke provides a straightforward, 'official' account of Llewellyn's career and intellectual development. Then the late Professor Grant Gilmore, a drafting partner of Llewellyn's and a key figure in the Code project, provides a personal testimonial in honor of Llewellyn. Finally, the third selection comes from a team of contemporary researchers who obtained access to Llewellyn's personal letters and unfinished manuscripts. They provide a fascinating and searing portrait of Llewellyn as a brilliant, turbulent, and troubled man, plagued by doubts and personal problems.

Biography of Karl Llewellyn
David Ray Papke[1]

Llewellyn, Karl Nickerson (22 May 1893–13 Feb. 1962), legal theorist and law reformer, was born in Seattle, Washington, the son of William Henry Llewellyn, a businessman of Welsh ancestry, and Janet George, an ardent Congregationalist and late Victorian reformer. His mother marched for woman suffrage and for Prohibition, and Llewellyn inherited her vigor and intelligence. Not long after Llewellyn's birth, his family moved to Brooklyn, where he attended Boys' High School. When Llewellyn was sixteen, his father decided his son would benefit from a period in Germany. He was enrolled in the Real gymnasium at Schwerin in Mecklenburg, where he became fully bilingual, a skill that would allow him later to publish in both English and German.

Llewellyn completed his secondary education in 1911, briefly attended the University of Lausanne, and in the fall of 1911 entered

---

1. David Ray Papke, "Karl Llewellyn," *American National Biography*, edited by John Garraty, vol 13 (New York: Oxford University Press, 1999), Copyright 1999 by the American Council of Learned Societies. Used by permission of Oxford University Press, Inc.

Yale College. He was an honors student and, despite his slight physical stature, avidly took up boxing. In 1914 he left Yale and studied for four months at the Sorbonne. When World War I began, the fondness Llewellyn had developed in Mecklenburg for German culture and discipline led him to join the German army. As a member of the Seventy-eighth Prussian Infantry, he was wounded near Ypres and spent three months in a military hospital. In February 1915 he was awarded the Iron Cross.

When Llewellyn returned to the United States in 1915, he completed his studies at Yale College and enrolled at the Yale Law School. He complained that the war had deprived the school of many superior students, and he was friendlier not with his classmates but with his instructors, in particular Arthur Corbin and Wesley Hohfeld. Earning an L.L.B. in 1918 and a J.D. in 1920, he graduated near the top of his class and served as editor in chief of the *Yale Law Journal*. He was invited to join the faculty on a part-time basis to teach commercial law and jurisprudence, subjects that would dominate throughout his subsequent career. He also offered a course in the Department of Anthropology and Sociology named "Law in Society."

Llewellyn worked during the early 1920s in the legal department of the National City Bank in New York City and in the Wall Street law firm of Shearman and Sterling. In 1924 he married Elizabeth Sanford. For ten years the Yale Law School held open an office for him to join its faculty on a full-time basis, but accommodating the preferences of his wife, Llewellyn in 1924 became a visiting lecturer at Columbia Law School and the following year became a full-time associate professor there.

At Columbia, Llewellyn was on the losing side in an internal power struggle concerning the designation of a new dean in 1928. He stayed on nevertheless, saying the school needed him now more than ever. Faculty colleagues and students apparently were of two minds about him. Some considered him brash, insensitive and unpredictable; others found him spirited, brilliant, and creative. A later faculty colleague probably captured Llewellyn best when he described him as an "extraordinary piece of radioactive material."

In the years 1929–1930 Llewellyn rose dramatically from the ranks of American law professors to the very top of his profession. He was appointed the first Betts Professor of Jurisprudence at Columbia, and he published in rapid succession two much-discussed volumes, *Cases and Materials in the Law of Sales* (1930) and *The Bramble Bush* (1930).

Almost 1,100 pages in length, *Cases and Materials in the Law of Sales* was a goundbreaking text that eschewed the conceptualism and emphasis on general principles that had previously reigned in the subject area. Llewellyn proffered instead historical materials, detailed analyses, and the digests of literally hundreds of often contradictory cases. His goal was to explode the bogus unity of sales law.

The Bramble Bush grew out of a series of lectures Llewellyn gave to first-year students. His shortest but most-read work, the volume warned against teaching and studying law as if it were merely a matter of established rules. Rules, or formal prescriptions and proscriptions of the state, could be important in predicting what a judge would do, but he added, "That is all their importance, except as pretty playthings." To emphasize rules above all else ran the risk of "developing the technician at the cost of the whole man."

The two volumes and a dozen articles, including "A Realistic Jurisprudence: 'The Next Step'" in the *Columbia Law Review* (1930), established Llewellyn as a leader of the "legal realist" movement. Although multifaceted and less coherent than a unified jurisprudence theory, legal realism in general called for the study of law not on the page but rather in action. What was important, the realists insisted, was the actual handling of disputes and negotiations by police, lawyers, judges, and citizens. In Llewellyn's opinion, the movement never meant to be a philosophy. Legal realism, he felt, was at its core "a methodology."

Despite a painful divorce from his first wife in 1930 and recurrent struggles with alcoholism, Llewellyn remained extremely productive during the pre-World War II years. In 1933 he married Emma Corstvet; they adopted a son. His provocative *The Cheyenne Way* (1941), coauthored with anthropologist E. Adamson Hoebel, was a major contribution to the anthropological study of primitive law. Contemplating the Cheyenne approach to law, Llewellyn said later, enabled him to put aside the assumption that law and justice stood inherently in conflict.

During World War II and after, Llewellyn turned his attention increasingly to the drafting and promotion of the Uniform Commercial Code, an effort to standardize American commercial law sponsored jointly by the American Law Institute and the National Conference of Commissioners on Uniform State Laws. He was chief reporter for the massive project, and although he worked with dozens of others, few doubted his influence. Scholar Grant Gilmore said, "Make no mistake: this Code was Llewellyn's Code; there is not a section, there is hardly a line, which does not bear his stamp and impress; from the beginning to end he inspired, directed and controlled it." The first [integrated] draft of the code was completed by 1949. Fifteen states formally adopted it before Llewellyn's death, and in subsequent years thirty-four more states adopted it. It was, stated simply, one of the most successful and pervasive law reforms in American legal history.

Consistent with Llewellyn's earlier disdain for conceptualism and rule-driven system building, the Code used loose, open-ended language. Article Two concerned the law of sales and looked in particular to questions of fact, reasonableness, good faith, and usage of trade for answers to legal controversies. The commercial community was approached almost as modern day Cheyenne and was trusted to derive legal fairness from its own norms.

Llewellyn divorced his second wife in 1946 and that same year married Soia Mentschikoff, who had been his student, research assistant, and associate chief reporter on the Uniform Commercial Code project. In 1951 he resigned from Columbia, where, because of his difficult and demanding personality, his relationship with faculty colleagues and the school administration had deteriorated badly. Llewellyn and Mentschikoff accepted a joint appointment at the University of Chicago Law School, the first time a major American law school had appointed spouses to its faculty.

A particular reason for Llewellyn's move to Chicago was his admiration for Dean Edward Levi, whose talents in Llewellyn's opinion would enable the University of Chicago Law School to compete with prestigious eastern schools. Levi thought just as highly of Llewellyn and Mentschikoff. The two energized the school and raised its scholarly standards. They held weekly parties at their home, inviting all students to attend, and many later cited their contacts with Llewellyn and Mentschikoff as the high points of their legal educations.

In 1960 Llewellyn published his magnum opus, *The Common Law Tradition: Deciding Appeals*. Echoing the skepticism concerning rules in his earlier scholarship, he argued in this volume that rules alone do not decide cases. The law, he thought, was in perpetual motion, and in most appeals judges exercise judicial creativity. However, forces also channeled this creativity and prevented it from becoming mere arbitrariness.

Following the publication of *The Common Law Tradition*, Llewellyn planned to lecture in Germany and use his lecture series to synthesize his jurisprudential views. Unfortunately, poor health intervened, and he died in Chicago. One of the greatest figures of twentieth-century legal academics, Llewellyn uniquely combined originality and theoretical sophistication with a hands-on commitment to practical and enduring law reform.

Discussion Question: Think for a moment about Llewellyn's education, scholarship, and personality. And consider his then-unorthodox view that the formalism of contract law should not apply to a community of merchants who hold each other to flexible, informal, and changing rules and customs. Do you think that he was a good choice for Chief Reporter of the Code?

In Memoriam: Karl Llewellyn
Grant Gilmore[2]

I knew Karl Llewellyn during the last fifteen years of his life. During the first six of those years, I was a member of the staff which he assembled and directed in the drafting of the Uniform Commercial Code.

During all the years of work on the Code no one ever questioned Karl's encyclopedic knowledge of the broad areas of law encompassed in the Code. We quickly learned to appreciate the resourcefulness of his mind, his clarity in analysis, and his ingenuity in devising solutions to the apparently insoluble. Karl was a master at grasping, intuitively, the hidden areas of agreement which underlay the clash of argument and at constructing a synthesis which often brought an angry debate to harmonious conclusion. Himself a man of strong opinions, he showed himself astonishingly patient—even of stupidity—although his capacity for Christian charity could, on occasion, be tried to, and beyond, the breaking point. He had, more than any other man I have ever know, the ability to put aside his own preconceptions; there was no *parti pris*, no pride of authorship, no dogma-

2. Reprinted by permission of The Yale Law Journal Company and William S. Hein Company from The Yale Law Journal, vol. 71, page 813 (1962).

tism. Nor was there in Karl's willingness to explore new approaches to long-familiar problems any trace of weakness or irresoluteness; his eagerness to listen, and to learn, proceeded from a sure confidence in his own strength.

Karl Llewellyn was, as we all must be, a man of his time. We are prisoners both of the world around us and of ourselves; living is mostly a matter of building the prison walls within which we are to be confined and we use whatever materials come to hand. Fifty years earlier, or fifty years later, we would be different from what we are. Karl, with respect to his professional career, was, then, a man of the period 1920–1960.

He came to the law at a time when a tradition—the great tradition of classical jurisprudence—was in the process of being destroyed. He became an enthusiastic demolisher and remained, throughout his life, instinctively opposed to system-building. His considerable contribution to the jurisprudence of this century was not in the elaboration of formal patterns, of logical constructs, of generalized theory. His work will, I believe, be remembered for its flashing insights, for the brilliance of its intuitions, for the powerful, untidy surge of life that carries it forward.

I do not know to what extent Karl would have accepted my characterization of his attitude toward systematic theory. There were moments and moods in which the building of systems attracted and exhilarated him. But there is manifest in his work a consistent, almost unconscious preference for the particular over the general. In the introduction of his casebook on Sales (1930) he wrote: "I do not conceive it to be a teacher's duty to let the true light shine." Light, surely, but the "true light" is quite another thing. In his great series of articles on the law of sales, which appeared during the 1930's, a recurrent theme is the need for "narrow issue" thinking, for abandoning, in the context of sales law, such "lump concepts" as that of title. A year or two ago Karl read over a short piece of mine on legal realism. His comment, I thought, illuminated both the nature of realism and the nature of his own thinking. "You go wrong," he said, "when you look at realism as a theory or a philosophy. It was neither. It was never meant to be either. What it was meant to be, and what it was, was a methodology."

I have perhaps overstated the destructive character of Karl's involvement with realism. It is easy enough to smash things. It is hard to destroy carefully, lovingly, precisely, only what needs to be destroyed, preserving what still has use. Karl's version of realism was affirmative, not negative, a labor of love and not of hate. He had a life-long love for the process and craft of judging, to which his last book bears eloquent witness. Appropriately, the title of that book repeats a phrase which we may take as a key to much of his work: The Common Law Tradition. Revolutionary as his early writings were thought to be, Karl abhorred abrupt departures, sudden breaks and the revealed certainty of novel illumination. He was a man of tradition, of continuity, of ordered growth and gradual change.

There may appear to be an element of paradox in my insistence on Karl's dislike of system-building, on his preference for the particular over the general, on his fascination with judge-made law. Over many years his energies were devoted to the drafting of statutes; this aspect of his work culminated in the fifteen-year ordeal of drafting the Uniform Commercial Code. Make no mistake: this Code was Llewellyn's Code; there is not a section, there is hardly a line, which does not bear his stamp and impress; from beginning to end he inspired, directed and controlled it. The statute-man, one assumes, must be, as I have said Karl was not, a system-builder, a generalizer, a despiser of the fumbling approximations of case law.

It was, I believe, Karl's non-systemic, particularizing cast of mind and his case-law orientation which gave to the statutes he drafted, and particularly to the Code, their profound originality. He was a remarkable draftsman and took a never-failing interest in even the minutiae of the trade. His instinct appeared to be to draft in a loose, open-ended style; his preferred solutions turned on questions of fact (reasonableness, good faith, usage of trade) rather than on rules of law. He had clearly in mind the idea of a case-law Code; one that would furnish guide-lines for a fresh start, would accommodate itself to changing circumstances, would not so much contain the law as free it for a new growth. The tastes of the practicing lawyers who advised the draftsmen were, in most cases, opposed to the flexible ideas of the Chief Reporter; they preferred, they insisted on, a tightly-drawn statute, precise, detailed and rigid. Among the many drafts of the Code which appeared, beginning in 1946, the early drafts were in many ways closer to Karl's conception of the Code than were the final drafts. In the concluding phase of the drafting, concessions were inevitably made to what might be called political pressures; I do not mean to suggest that these pressures were in any sense evil or malevolent. I have come to feel that Karl saw more clearly than his critics that the Code as he initially conceived it might better have served the purposes of the next fifty years. Yet Karl never lost sight of the fact that his job was to produce, not the best Code which could be produced by a band of scholarly angels, but the best Code which stood a chance of passage in the imperfect world of men. He cheerfully gave ground when he had to; the final product was indubitably his and will remain an enduring tribute to his memory.

We live in a world of yea-saying, a world in which whoever is not with us must be against us, a world in which whatever is not white must be black, a world in which, it may be, the true light shines. Karl Llewellyn was not a man for such a world. He was a man more given to questions than to answers, more taken with seeking than with finding. He loved beauty in all its many forms; he delighted in the infinite variety of things and people and ideas. He was not perfect; he was merely, in his many-faceted humanity, a strong and humble man, a man of great kindness and charity, a man of understanding, a man of wit—a man who came closer than most of us do, or will, to wisdom.

Discussion Question: Gilmore points to a tension within Llewellyn, namely that he was critical of abstract systems (such as the doctrinal thicket of contract law), yet he was the chief architect of a giant system, i.e., the Code. Gilmore suggests that Llewellyn negotiated this conflict by creating a system (the Code) which is very open-ended and therefore allows courts to resolve disputes by looking to real-world customs within the business community (as opposed to the prior law of commercial transactions, which focused on theoretical issues concerning which party held title, whether consideration had been given, and so forth, concerns which were unimportant to the participants in commercial transactions). A chief expression of Llewellyn's anti-formalism, as we have seen, is the expansive notion of "Agreement" to include usage of trade and course of dealing (see 1-201(3)), plus the requirements of good faith (1-203) and reasonableness (1-204). Do you think that Llewellyn provided a useful framework for commercial law while avoiding the problem of most system-builders, namely the creation of a beautiful system of abstract rules that are too divorced from practice?

Alcoholism and Angst in the Life and Work of Karl Llewellyn

James J. Connolly, Peggy Pschirrer, and Robert Whitman[3]

Succeeding generations of lawyers and legal scholars have been impressed by the work and the charismatic personality of Karl Llewellyn. This interest has always involved some combination of two elements: First, an appreciation of the importance of Llewellyn's theoretical and scholarly contributions, and second, a fascination with Llewellyn's boldly unconventional personal style. The thesis of this paper is that Karl Llewellyn was more than a brilliant eccentric and icon of American legal theory. He was a strikingly complex and chaotic individual whose personal upheaval was inseparable from his outlook and scholarship. He was also the product of the times in which he lived and worked. A full appreciation of Karl Llewellyn and his significance to legal thought requires an analysis of his scholarship within the context of the society he lived in and the personal and generational forces that helped to shape his tempestuous life and turbulent scholarship.

Llewellyn became an emotionally volatile alcoholic, plagued by severe feelings of sexual and professional failure... We use the term "angst" in this paper to describe the sum of Karl Llewellyn's self-doubts and his depression. The term "angst" is appropriate for the complex of painful personal experiences of this leading modernist intellectual. Despite his many accomplishments, Llewellyn saw himself as a fearful and avoidant person. He was tormented by a sense of being a sexual failure, and few of his legal accomplishments met his own high standards of achievement.

In today's psychiatric terminology, Llewellyn's sadness and self-doubt would probably be described as Dysthymic Disorder. In Llewellyn's time, his condition would likely have been described as neurotic depression. Such mild but chronic depressions are characterized by feelings of sadness and low self-esteem, and some sense of hopelessness. They may also be characterized by some disturbances of appetite, sleeping, or energy level. Dysthymic Disorder must be

---

3. James J. Connolly, Peggy Pschirrer, and Robert Whitman, Alcoholism and Angst in the Life and Work of Karl Llewellyn, 24 Ohio N. L. Rev. 43 (1998). Reprinted by permission.

distinguished, however, from the acute condition now known as Major Depression, which would involve severe disruptions of appetite or sleep, loss of interest in typical activities, severe agitation or fatigue, inability to concentrate or make decisions, and recurrent thoughts of death or suicide.

Llewellyn's letters demonstrate that he suffered from the dysthymic symptoms of chronic sadness and low self-esteem as well as disturbed sleep. Llewellyn also periodically experienced feelings of hopelessness and disturbances of appetite and energy level. Some of Llewellyn's depressed affect might be seen as resulting from the effects of his overuse of alcohol, but the problem of self-esteem and general sadness goes farther and deeper. Indeed, Karl Llewellyn appears to have been the type of person in which mild (usually dysthymic or nondisabling) depression and a drinking problem reinforce each other. At least during some periods of the mid-1940s, however, Llewellyn appears to have suffered from an exacerbation of his emotional problems that could be considered to constitute Major Depression...

Early on, Llewellyn had burst upon the legal scene as a genius with great potential, but despite his initial prominence as a generational insurgent, the unfolding years of the New Deal caught Llewellyn off balance. He found that he was no longer leading the charge of his generation. Like other insurgent modernists of his generation, Llewellyn had throughout his early adulthood flaunted heavy use of alcohol as a principle flag of rebellion, and like many of the other aging modernists, Llewellyn gradually succumbed to alcoholism...

During the early 1930's, Llewellyn began his complicated second marriage, he failed in his quest for public office [in 1934 he ran for New York State Assembly as a Democrat but stepped down prior to the election], and his drinking habit grew worse. Llewellyn's intellectual and professional efforts redoubled in the face of what he saw as mounting setbacks and failure. He brought to this work of lawgiving the fervid and erratic brilliance captured in the tribal name given him by the Cheyenne Indians during his anthropological field-work: "Fire Gets Away." Llewellyn went through repeated treatments for his alcoholism, experienced bouts of depression and serious marital problems, and conducted an illicit love affair with his foremost student and disciple, Soia Mentschikoff. In 1945–46, Llewellyn experienced a profound crisis that affected every aspect of his life. [The authors quote from Llewellyn's letters in which he admits sexual dysfunction in connection with his second wife Emma, and discusses his repeated attempts to control alcoholism. Llewellyn's personal problems culminated in various troubling incident in 1945–6, during which time Llewellyn offered his resignation from Columbia Law School and was caught in a love triangle with his increasingly estranged second wife Emma and his former student Soia Mentschikoff. Yet the authors note that "Llewellyn was able to 'keep his act together' on the national level of the UCC process."] By the time (several years later) that Llewellyn's life became reasonable stable again, the insurgent had been lovingly transformed into Karl Llewellyn, the legal icon. He completed his academic work surveying a changed legal field, a Grand Old Man describing the apparent capture of the citadel by the forces he had once led in the attack, still drinking to reduce his sense of personal inadequacy...

Karl Llewellyn had a brilliant career as a legal scholar, but there was a canker on the rose. The canker was his very troubled personal existence, his alcoholism, his depression, his sexual and relationship problems. After a period of brilliant writing in the 1930s and early 1940s, Llewellyn had a very marked slump in creativity and productivity during the later 1940s. He rallied and reorganized after his move to University of Chicago in 1951, and his final work was a kind of intellectual reconciliation within American jurisprudence. Despite having paid a ferocious price in personal terms, Llewellyn ultimately fulfilled on his early promise as a legal scholar...

Karl Llewellyn, one of the greatest American legal scholars of the twentieth century, was a chronic alcoholic, consistently plagued by self-doubt, intermittently depressed, and quite unhappy in his relationships. One must consider these painful aspects of his life and those of his contemporaries if one is to understand Llewellyn and his times, but more importantly to understand the progression of his thought. Unique personal and generational struggles gave rise to his special insights about the origins of law in social life, and his enthusiasms for seeking the essence of law in the raw, the fresh, and the primitive. Over the course of his adult life, his scholarship first reflected impulses to overthrow or to escape, then shifted to advocacy of group autonomy and self-regulation. Finally, his insights moved toward reconciliation with, and rejuvenation of the American judicial system as a whole. These three phases of his scholarship corresponded to three phases in his professional relations, first as a leader of a generational insurgency, second as the politically humbled but ardent researcher in the law-ways of American Indians and American merchants, third as Grand Old Man who achieved a new lease on life after his earlier way of life unraveled. He played out all three roles well enough to ensure that he has a permanent place in American legal history.

Discussion Question: After reading this selection, you may feel like you know too much about Karl Llewellyn. Is this information about his depression, sexual dysfunction, and alcoholism somehow relevant to our understanding of the Code?

Chapter Four

Methodology of the Code

The readings in this chapter address the question of whether the Code adopts a particular philosophical orientation that runs through its various provisions like a guiding thread. Obviously, if there is such a unifying principle (or principles), its discovery could strengthen uniformity by ensuring that courts approach the Code with a common understanding of its fundamental commitments.

In the first reading, Professor Danzig argues that the underlying philosophy of the Code is to be found in Llewellyn's belief that every fact pattern contains an imminent logic that suggests an appropriate resolution. By requiring the parties to comply with open-ended terms such as "reasonableness," "good faith," and "usage of trade," Llewellyn effectively vested judges with the power to declare the specific requirements of the commercial law (i.e., to say what "commercially reasonable" actually means in a given context). Danzig points out the dangers in this approach, namely that it tends to valorize the existing customs and trade usages of the marketplace (even if they are unfair), and it undermines the Code's professed uniformity by vesting judges of diverse political dispositions with so much power to declare the law. Finally, it forces commercial lawyers to focus heavily on case decisions to flesh-out the meaning of open-ended terms, thereby eliminating the efficiency and simplicity that a Code might offer if it was sufficiently detailed.

In the second reading, Professor Gedid argues that the Code is best understood as a Legal Realist statute, owing to Llewellyn's involvement with that movement. As a Realist, Llewellyn was impressed with the ability of judges to 'make' law through freewheeling interpretations, so he sought to constrain the exercise of unprincipled judicial lawmaking. Gedid focuses on two of Llewellyn's underlying philosophies that operate as constraints on the judiciary. First, Llewellyn insisted that each Code provision (as well as the Code itself) should have a particular purpose and policy, which might be referred to as a 'patent reason' (in this regard, you might see Official Comment 1 to Section 1-102: "This Act should be construed in accordance with its underlying purposes and policies"). Second,

Llewellyn specifically sought a *code* format as opposed to a series of uniform laws dealing with various aspects of commercial law. The two innovations (the patent reason device and the adoption of a code format) aid in uniformity because they place limits on how a court should construe a Code provision, e.g., a court should first look at the principles underlying the specific provision at issue and then to the overall principles running throughout the Code as a whole before venturing outside to the amorphous common law of contracts and to other sources.

Finally, Professor Gregory Maggs suggests that Llewellyn's vision of the Code is becoming increasingly diffuse as the Code goes through a seemingly interminable revision process. In particular, Llewellyn's penchant for open-ended provisions is being supplanted by a strict exactitude and literalness that is out of keeping with Llewellyn's vision of the Code as a flexible framework that can change with the evolution of business practices.

The Jurisprudence of the Uniform Commercial Code
Richard Danzig[1]

The central argument of this Essay is that Article 2 of the UCC is an idiosyncratic piece of legislation because in critical provisions it neither pretends to the substance nor adopts the form of the usual legislative enactment. It is suggested that an appreciation of the jurisprudential theories of the Article's principal drafter makes the unusual aspects of the Code's approach more salient and more understandable. And it is argued that the animating principle behind these theories and this legislative achievement is, paradoxically, and, in some respects unwisely, a renunciation of legislative responsibility and power.

At the outset it should be noted, however, that some of the peculiarities of the Code derive as much from the atypical nature of the problems and persons with which it deals as from the unusual character of Llewellyn's view of the legal process. Commercial law is at the margin of public law. It deals with a subcommunity ("merchants"), whose members occupy a status position distinct from soci-

---

1. Richard Danzig, A Comment on the Jurisprudence of the Uniform Commercial Code, 27 Stan. L. Rev. 621 (1975). Reprinted by permission.

ety at large, whose disputes are often resolved by informal negotiation or in private forums, whose relationships tend to continue over time rather than ending with the culmination of single transactions, and whose primary rules derive from a sense of fairness widespread—if imprecisely defined—within the commercial community. In this situation the legislature (often ignorant of the actual circumstances that control commerce) is not likely to conceive of itself as the arena for negotiation between competing interest groups; it is not likely, in fact, to see itself as a place where anything is decided. Instead, it often may merely articulate and place the state's imprimatur on private arrangements, fabricated outside its halls. It would not be altogether surprising, then, to find that the legislative process associated with the Uniform Commercial Code was more like law-stating than law-making.

The uniformity sought by the Act's proponents undoubtedly further limited the opportunities for legislative activism and even contributed to some of the idiosyncracies of the legislation's form. If the Code were to be widely adopted, it would have to be easily assimilated into the prevailing ideology and the prevailing law. Individual legislatures were particularly urged to restrict their lawmaking propensities, at least as to enactments within the framework of this Act, and they were restrained from generating a unique legislative history by the prepackaged gloss provided in the form of official commentary.

Characteristics such as these which stem from a code that would be both uniform and commercial suggest that there is more at play in Article 2 than Llewellyn's jurisprudence. But this Essay suggests that Llewellyn's jurisprudential preferences strongly reinforced these situational factors and that the genius of the Code is derived in large measure from the mesh Llewellyn effected between the pragmatic demands he faced and the jurisprudential views he held...

Instead of regarding law as a body of deduced rules, or as an instrument chosen by social planners from among a universe of alternatives, Llewellyn saw law as an articulation and regularization of unconsciously evolved mores—as a crystallization of a generally recognized and almost indisputably right rule (a "singing reason"), inherent in, but very possibly obscured by, existing patterns of relationships. To him, an "immanent law" lay embedded in any situation and the task of the law authority was to discover it. In perhaps the key passage in *The Common Law Tradition*, Llewellyn quotes Levin Goldschmidt with approval:

> Every fact-pattern of common life, so far as the legal order can take it in, carries within itself its appropriate, natural rules, its right law. This is a natural law which is real, not imaginary; it not a creature of mere reason, but rests on the solid foundation of what reason can recognize in the nature of man and of the life conditions of the time and place; it is thus not eternal or changeless nor everywhere the same, but is indwelling in the very circumstances of life. The highest task of law-giving consists in uncovering and implementing this immanent law.

This view has strikingly negative implications for an active legislative role. If law exists and needs only to be discovered, it is not necessary or helpful (but indeed probably only burdensome) that the law-articulating agency be democratically elected and politically responsive; to proceed effectively, a lawmaker needs only a capacity for detecting the "situation sense" and a good faith commitment to the exercise of that capacity. Moreover, since law is immanent in "the very circumstances" of time and place, the agency best suited to find it is presumably not one of general inquiry and decision, like a legislature, but rather one with a more particularized insight: that is, a court should declare war by a careful review of "trouble cases" (disputes)...

Article 2 of the Code can profitably be viewed as adapting the philosophy of "immanent law" to a specific context. Just as Llewellyn found the "Cheyenne Way" by the method of value-free observation, Article 2 frequently speaks as though courts should discover the law merchant from a careful, disinterested examination of custom and fact situations. Article 2 is not, in the main, an example of legislative lawmaking, it is a guide to law-finding. It does not tell judges the law; it tells them how to find the law. The law is found not in doctrine, not in policy, but in directed exploration of the "fact-pattern of common life." The search is for the "natural law...of the life conditions of the time and place..." Consider, for example, the "law" promulgated by Uniform Commercial Code, section 2-609:

Right to Adequate Assurance of Performance

(1)...When reasonable grounds for insecurity arise with respect to the performance of either party the other may in writing demand adequate assurance of due performance and until he receives such assurance may if commercially reasonable suspend any performance for which he has not already received the agreed return.

(2)...Between merchants the reasonableness of grounds for insecurity and the adequacy of any assurance offered shall be determined according to commercial standards.

In a 1944 draft of this section Llewellyn offered a comment (later omitted) that is revealing as to his aim and method: "Subsection 2 is technically unnecessary.... But there are a number of lines of doctrine in regard to what constitutes a breach, or even an excuse, which make it vital to remind that the intention of this Act is to use the standards not of past decisions but of current commerce."

In telling a court to use current "commercial standards" to determine when "reasonable grounds" for insecurity exist, or to assess whether "adequate assurance" or something more excessive is requested, or to decide if supervision of performance is "commercially reasonable," this provision—which is typical of Article 2—is doing neither more nor less than asking a court to find "the immanent laws" of "the time and place."

As another example of this jurisprudential perspective, consider the much-discussed unconscionability clause of the UCC:

(1) If the court as a matter of law finds the contract or any clause of the contract to have been unconscionable at the time it was made the court may refuse to enforce the contract, or it may enforce the remainder of the contract without the unconscionable clause, or it may so limit the application of any unconscionable clause as to avoid any unconscionable result.

(2) When it is claimed or appears to the court that the contract or any clause thereof may be unconscionable the parties shall be afforded a reasonable opportunity to present evidence as to its commercial setting, purpose and effect to aid the court in making the determination.

Many have noted that this section tells a court almost nothing save that unconscionability is bad and this it exists. But these critics tend to treat it as an aberration—as the product of a lapse or of a too frequently compromised drafting procedure. A jurisprudential perspective on the whole of Article 2 would suggest that section 2-302 provides a naked example of a very general phenomenon. To those who see the legislature as an engine of social reform, the vacuity of the clause is woefully disturbing. But if the weight of lawmaking is thought best distributed elsewhere, then the clause serves its purpose. It empowers and directs the courts to [in Llewellyn's words,] "absorb the particular trouble and resolve it each time into a new, usefully guiding, forward-looking, felt standard-for-action or even rule-of-law" ...

The rhetoric surrounding the Sales Article is strikingly amoral. Llewellyn spoke about the Code, and Article 2 is written, as though the insights required for this lawmaking job were not born of any reflection on the gap between the real and ideal, but rather through the acquisition of intimate familiarity with "current commerce." Thus in his [initial memorandum to the NCCUSL in support of the Code] Llewellyn spoke of the Code as a means of regularizing "a very considerable body of commercial law which is very largely non-political in character." And the beginning of the Code echoes this orientation by cataloguing the "underlying purposes and policies of this Act" as:

> (a) to simplify, clarify and modernize the law governing commercial transaction;
>
> (b) to permit the continued expansion of commercial practice through custom, usage and agreement of the parties;
>
> (c) to make uniform the law among the various jurisdictions.

Taken on the basis of these pretensions, one might suppose that the Code belies Llewellyn's defense of realism—the second step seems never to come. In fact, however, the situation is more complicated than that. The Code is not oblivious to ethical concerns. However clearly section 2-302 signals a legislative void, by its very existence it evidences the draftsman's commitment to the notion that a moral referent is relevant in adjudication. What the clause lacks in legislative prescription it charges the judge to provide by other means.

It is the choice of means that is troublesome. The Code appears to be predicated on an assumption that perception of an ideal can be effected by the same "technology" used to secure an appreciation of the real. Ethical questions are relevant, but they are regarded as posing problems of discovery rather than choice. The premise appears to be that values have an objectively ascertainable existence and a near universal acceptance and thus can be judicially discovered just as a "reasonable price" can be ascertained by reference to a market.

Thus, for example, if a seller is charged with breaching an implied warranty of fitness for a particular purpose, the courts are directed by section 2-316(3)(c) to assess a claimed exclusion of the warranty according to contemporary usage, and usage is to be discovered, according to section 1-205, Comment 5, by attention to the mores "currently observed by the great majority of decent dealers, even though dissidents ready to cut corners do not agree." Who are "commercially decent dealers?" What, at the margins, are the indices of decency and indecency? What if "decent" practices, as a judge perceives them, are not those of the "great majority," but instead those of the dissidents? The presumption appears to be that what is "commercially decent" and what is "unconscionable," what is "good faith" and what is bad faith, what is good law and what is bad law will be self-evident in one who carefully studies the situation. It is apparently an axiom of this approach that "good law" cannot be described for courts, but they will know it when they see it.

This approach is disturbing on several counts. First, insofar as the approach is workable, it tends to confine the impact of the law to a reaffirmation of the predominant morals of the marketplace. Practices well below the market's moral median may be constrained, but sine the median is the standard, by definition, it will be unaffected. Further, this approach seems to encourage exactly that which "realism" was supposed to discourage: a projection of a judge's values onto the scene before him, and then a "discovery" of them as though they existed in an objectively determinable way. The Code approach marks critical choices as technical assessments and allocates them to decision makers (judges) of low visibility and low responsibility from the standpoint of the larger public...Beyond this, because assessments of reasonableness, unconscionability, materiality, and the like can be expected to vary unpredictably from judge to judge, the Llewellyn approach seems paradoxically to undermine that very certainty and consistency in the law the Uniform Commercial Code was dedicated to obtaining.

Lastly, an emphasis on the discovery of moral propositions is costly because it tends to focus attention on those considerations which are salient for the parties at hand, at the expense of attention to larger concerns of which the disputants are perhaps unconscious.

That is, the methodology itself encourages lawmakers to see law as Pound feared— "as a body of devices for the purposes of business instead of as a body of means toward general social ends."

It could be argued that so narrow a perspective is peculiarly appropriate for a code dealing with the law of contracts. If private vices make public virtues, the maximizing lawmaker may do well to keep his concepts of utility to himself, leaving the parties free to determine their own course. But such a view is by no means compelled by the subject matter. [L]lewellyn himself conceded the importance of a wider perspective. The preface to his casebook on sales acknowledges that "[T]he book errs, I think, in too happily assuming the needs of buyers and sellers to be the needs of the community, and in rarely reaching beyond business practice in evaluation of legal rules" . . .

Article 2 is rife with such open-ended words (none of them referred to in the definitional section) as "reasonable time," "reasonable medium," "reasonable grounds," even "reasonable price," "reasonable value," "fair and reasonable cause," and "material alter[ation]," as well as the notorious "unconscionability." The use of generalized guides to decision (for example, custom and usage) and open-ended terms (reasonableness, good faith, unconscionable), the injection of "official commentary" declaring the intent of the drafters, and, above all, the scarcity of provisions explicit enough to be applied without a consideration of circumstances, compel a court that would use the Code to move beyond the literalism of "mechanical jurisprudence" . . . Llewellyn has drafted a statute that minimizes the differences between the ways courts and legislatures operate. He has delegated legislative decisions to courts, and has phrased a piece of legislation that, save for its comprehensiveness, reads very much like a judicial opinion.

This derogation of the legislative function appears to be premised on the triad of dubious assumptions that self-evident ideal resolutions of situational problems exist, that they can be discovered by careful scrutiny of actual situations, and that once articulated they will be widely accepted.

It is suggested here that the animating theory of Article 2 is that law is immanent. The law job is to search it out. There is thus no need for a legislature to create law. The central focus, as in all the writings of the realists, is on courts. Article 2 is a document whose thrust is not so much to put law on the statute books as it is to coerce courts into looking for law in life.

Discussion Question: Danzig argues that while the Code is a statutory enactment and would therefore seem to vest control of commercial transactions in the legislative branch, it nevertheless vests *courts* with the dominant power to declare the law by virtue of containing fact-specific notions that can only be determined on a case-by-case basis in a court of law, such as usage of trade, good faith, reasonableness, and so on. Llewellyn thought that this approach would not lead to inconsistent decisions, so long as the courts are willing to follow the animating principles and policies set forth clearly in the Official Comments. In your opinion, can the Code maximize court discretion without sacrificing uniformity, or do you think that the open-ended provisions of the Code will inevitably lead to non-uniformity?

U.C.C. Methodology: Taking A Realistic Look At The Code
John L. Gedid[2]

Recently, critics of the Uniform Commercial Code have proposed either revisions or federal enactment of the Code. These critics have perceived the Code as failing to produce uniformity, thereby creating unpredictable case law. Some commentators blame these problems on textual ambiguity in the Code, whereas others suggest that Code language is inconsistent. If such lack of uniformity exists, however, its principal cause is the failure to employ a standard or uniform methodology for both interpreting and applying the Code...

Llewellyn's approach to the Code involved the use of two techniques: [1] the use of the code form, and [2] a particular drafting style that grew out of his theory of statutory interpretation [namely, the 'patent reason' technique discussed below].

First, Llewellyn's choice of the code form in revising commercial law had important methodological consequences. This Article will develop the thesis that a code requires a special methodology for interpretation simply because it is generically a code rather than a "normal" statute. Although continental legal thinkers associate code methodology with a different set of interpretational devices that are

2. John L. Gedid, U.C.C. Methodology: Taking a Realistic Look at the Code, 29 Wlm. & Mary L. Rev. 341 (1988). Reprinted by permission of the author and the William & Mary Law Review.

part of the civil law, this Essay does not advocate continental or civil law methodology for Code interpretation. The author's position is that the structure and form of codes make them different in kind from most other statutes, thereby requiring a different methodology of interpretation. In the case of the Code, not only did Llewellyn choose that particular form, but he joined it to his new legal realist theory of statutory drafting and interpretation. The resulting Code is utterly unique, even among codes.

Second, Llewellyn's articles, memoranda, and speeches disclose the evolution of a general theory about statutory interpretation and the legal process. Llewellyn's drafting style evolved from his theories about law and the legal process. His drafting included a definite set of objectives, values, and procedural assumptions about statutory interpretation and application. These assumptions, objectives, and values did not enter the Code indirectly or covertly; Llewellyn expressly and purposely incorporated them in his drafting efforts. The Code is thus the first and perhaps the only statute that incorporates legal realist notions of statutory drafting and interpretation. *It is the first legal realist statute.* Legal realism, through Llewellyn, produced the most distinctive feature of the Code: a new, utterly unique methodology. If the legal profession and the courts recognize and adopt that methodology, much of the nonuniformity and unpredictability in judicial decisions interpreting the Code will disappear...

Judicial decisions have largely ignored the realist methodology that Llewellyn incorporated into the Code. The failure of the courts to follow a uniform method of interpretation and application of the Code has been a major cause of nonuniformity or inconsistency in Code decisions. Llewellyn understood the difficulties of statutory interpretation and realized that courts would be unwilling to give up ingrained methods of interpreting statutes. He attempted to resolve these problems by using two devices in tandem in drafting the Code—the code form and the patent reason drafting technique. These devices grew out of his efforts to analyze past statutory interpretational methodology and its inadequacies, and to produce a realist theory of statutory interpretation. Llewellyn attempted to accomplish a critique of existing statutory interpretational methodology and to generate a constructive new theory to replace or improve it. His effort was deliberately analogous to the analysis and suggestions made by the legal realists in connection with the judicial process in nonstatutory cases, in which the courts construed pure case precedent. He employed these two devices within his own realist framework. The assumptions of legal realism thus were major influences in the drafting of the Code.

Many implications for Code interpretational methodology flow from the use of the patent reason device and the code form. First, the use of the code form has significance for interpretation. A debate has raged over the differences between continental methods of interpreting a code and the common law methods of interpreting a statute. Without regard for any of the systemic or theoretic considerations urged in that debate, however, the mere use of the code form leads to several unavoidable methodological requirements. These requirements are inherent in the code form itself.

The Code was drafted as an integrated, unified whole. This drafting philosophy led to extensive cross-references and relationships among the text and comments of the various sections, parts, groups of sections, and articles. Code methodology must recognize this textual unity. In interpreting and applying the Code, the usual focus should not be on single sections viewed in isolation. Because of the integrated code approach, many terms, concepts, definitions, principles, and rules explain and supplement each other. As a result, examination of a concept, rule, or policy must involve the use and relationship of that concept in the several contexts in which it appears in the context of the usually related group of sections in which it appears, in the wider context of the Code part in which it appears, in the context of general obligations, right, and policies imposed by the Code, and in the context of the other sections that, although in different parts of the Code, nevertheless refer to the section being construed or to a closely related concept. Although these observations seem obvious, many courts and commentators still refuse to acknowledge them.

Second, the use of the patent reason technique in drafting the Code has profound implications for Code interpretational methodology. The real importance of the patent reason technique is apparent when the interpreter compares the Code approach to the use of policy with the use that legislatures and courts ordinarily make of statutory policy. Legislatures commonly incorporate a general statement of purpose, policy, or reason into the preamble or definitional part of a statute. Courts may then use these general statements in interpreting the statute. In the Code's patent reason technique, however,

Llewellyn used purpose and policy in a totally different fashion. In drafting the Code, Llewellyn continuously and consistently employed policy and purpose as the central device to convey and clarify statutory meaning. As a result, purpose, policy, and reason are major determinants of what the language of the text means. This active use of policy should be contrasted with the use made of policy as part of a canon of construction when courts construe a typical, noncode statute.

The patent reason principle also assigns a definite role to the courts in interpreting and applying the open-ended principles of the Code. Llewellyn used the patent reason technique because of his realist understanding of the judicial process of statutory interpretation. He recognized that the courts have some leeway in interpreting a statute. He also recognized that this leeway is similar to the latitude courts employ in using case precedents in decisions that do not involve a statute. His objective was to give guidance to courts in exercising this leeway. The patent reason concept in the Code thus embodies realist theory about the way courts function.

Although commentators have complained about lack of uniformity in Code decisions since its enactment, they have also demonstrated little understanding of the procedural and methodological devices used to construct the Code. The combination of realist jurisprudence and Llewellyn's drafting techniques resulted in a totally unique product that is, perhaps, the first "realist" statute. Use of policy, purpose, and reason in interpreting the Code according to the drafter's design, along with the use of a relational approach to interpretation, which the code form inherently requires, will go far to produce the uniform results Llewellyn sought.

Discussion Question: Do you agree with Gedid that proper understanding and application of the patent reason device and the code format will effectively promote uniformity, or do you believe that the open-ended provisions of the Code will inevitably lead to inconsistent rulings by judges with diverse agendas? For example, does the open-ended test for "unconscionability" in Section 2-302 leave too much discretion in the hands of judges to allow or strike contracts as they see fit, or do you feel that judges are adequately constrained by the purposes set out in the Official Comments and in the related provisions of the Code?

Karl Llewellyn's Fading Imprint on The Jurisprudence of the Uniform Commercial Code
Gregory E. Maggs[3]

The UCC at one time indisputably owed more to Professor Karl Llewellyn than to anyone else. Although Llewellyn did not initiate the plan to combine various uniform state laws on business subjects into a coherent code, he played a pivotal role in translating this objective into the UCC. Llewellyn led the UCC's drafting as the "Chief Reporter" from 1942 until his death in 1962. He and his wife, Professor Soia Mentschikoff, also served as reporters for three of the nine "articles"—or principal parts—of the UCC. Throughout this process, Llewellyn consistently strived to make the UCC distinct from other statutes and laws by imbuing it with features that reflected his deeply held juridical beliefs. For these reasons, the UCC has acquired nicknames like "Karl's Kode" and "Lex Llewellyn."

Llewellyn was a leader of the Legal Realist movement that emerged in this country during the 1920s and 1930s. Scholars associated with this school of jurisprudence did not agree on everything, but they all held an intense interest in understanding what actually influences judges when they decide cases. As discussed more fully within, some of the Legal Realists, including Llewellyn, shared a prescriptive vision for crafting legislation. They believed that statutes should seek to improve judicial decisions by recognizing that judges inevitably act with considerable discretion, and by seeking to guide this discretion rather than futilely attempting to eliminate it.

When Llewellyn set to work on the UCC project, he naturally wanted to implement his jurisprudential ideas. Llewellyn succeeded in giving the UCC at least five important features inspired by Legal Realism. In particular, as a result of his influence, the UCC:

* favored open-ended standards over firm rules;

* avoided formalities;

* required and facilitated the "purposive interpretation" of its provisions;

---

3. Gregory E. Maggs, Karl Llewellyn's Fading Imprint on the Jurisprudence of the Uniform Commercial Code, 71 U. Colo. L. Rev. 541 (2000). Reprinted with permission of the University of Colorado Law Review.

* did not attempt to provide an exclusive statement of the law, but instead directed courts to supplement its rules with general legal and equitable principles; and

* provided a range of remedies that principally served to make injured parties whole.

In recent years, the UCC has undergone considerable expansion and revision. Article 2A on leases of goods and Article 4A on funds transfers have been added. Articles 2A, 3, 4, 5, 6, 8, and 9 have been extensively revised. Moreover, drafts of new versions of Articles 1, 2, and 2A are currently in the works.

This article contends that these substantial additions and revisions have done more than merely alter and augment the legal rules in the UCC. They have had the additional effect of diminishing Llewellyn's jurisprudential contributions. The modern drafters and revisers of the UCC have not strived to retain the five legislative features identified above. Indeed, in some instances, they specifically have rejected them and the philosophy behind them...

[Maggs identifies the distinctive jurisprudential features of the Code, most notably its favoring of open-ended standards instead of rigid rules, its rejection of the formalism in common law contract doctrine, its promotion of 'purposive interpretation' by providing judges with statements of purpose and policy underlying the provisions, its non-exclusivity in permitting courts to supplement the code with common law principles, and its remedy sections which concentrate on making the aggrieved party whole. Maggs then nicely illustrates how these features have been eroded in successive versions of the Code].

The foregoing discussion attempted to document how Llewellyn's influence on the jurisprudence of the UCC is diminishing. Many of the original goals that he and others worked to accomplish have faded. The UCC now relies more on formalities. Complete and specific statements of the law have become more common, with reliance on standards and purposive interpretation diminishing. The drafters of the new and revised articles have attempted to make them more exclusive, and remedies presently serve purposes other than compensation for loss.

What has caused Llewellyn's imprint to fade? No doubt it would be dramatic and also intellectually satisfying to identify a single person, interest group, or idea as the impetus for all of the changes in the

UCC's jurisprudence. This question, however, does not have a simple answer. As the foregoing discussion indicates, many separate revisions have occurred. These revisions have taken place over a period of about a dozen years. Numerous individuals, including consumer and business advocates, academics, and government representatives, had their hands in most of them. As a result, a wide variety of factors probably brought about the changes in the UCC's jurisprudence.

One partial hypothesis is that change has occurred because of the considerable practical experience with the UCC that has accumulated over the past fifty years. Many lawyers and judges have found the UCC difficult to understand. Whether correctly or incorrectly, the drafters may have concluded that purposive interpretation, open-ended standards, the elimination of formalities, and the use of supplemental general principles tend to create confusion. They have opted for what they consider more straightforward ways of expressing the law.

Another hypothesis that explains some of the change is that the law and economics movement has changed the way many legal scholars evaluate legal rules. In particular, nearly everyone now thinks more carefully about how the law can create incentives that will affect behavior. Perhaps for this reason, as noted above, the drafters of the new articles and the various revisions have seen that remedies may serve purposes besides compensation.

A third hypothesis is that, in the decades between the original drafting of the UCC and its large-scale revision in the past ten or fifteen years, trust in judges has diminished among the business community. The perception of judicial activism in constitutional and statutory interpretation may have contributed to this feeling. Whatever the cause, subsequent reformers have not shared Llewellyn's optimism that judges will strive to reach correct results. As noted above, banks and industry groups have played a larger role in drafting the law. Unlike Llewellyn, they have seen a need to corral wayward judges.

A fourth hypothesis is that Llewellyn's jurisprudential influence has faded to some extent because the textualist school of statutory interpretation has become very influential. This school emphasizes that judges should follow legislative commands as expressed in statutes, and should limit their consideration of other factors. To some, principles of textualism lead to the correlative view that legislatures should take responsibility for making the law, and should not delegate the task to judges. Purposive interpretation, open-ended standards, and supplemental general principles do not fit well into this model.

Finally, business practices or our knowledge of them may well have changed in the past fifty years. Undeniably, the marketplace has become less localized and more competitive. For example, a bank located in one city may compete with banks in other cities in issuing letters of credit, certificates of deposit, cashier's checks, wire transfers, and other instruments governed by the UCC. This competition may lead to calls for clearer rules because each participant wants to know exactly what is permitted and what is not.

Determining the exact causes of the changes, or arguing for or against what has occurred, is simply beyond the scope of this article. Llewellyn and others involved in the UCC's creation strongly believed in their positions. The revisers of the UCC, on the other hand, apparently have seen reasons for adopting different approaches in many instances. This article makes only the claim that a change in the jurisprudence of the UCC has occurred...

If Llewellyn's theories had remained dominant, then the drafters of the UCC would not be adding formalities and replacing standards with rules. They would not be backing away from purposive interpretation, nonexclusivity, and the policy of using remedies solely for compensation. Perhaps this development suggests that attempting to maintain a single consistent jurisprudence in the UCC, or any major codification, for a long time is impossible. Our legal culture probably is too pluralistic for any one school of legal thought to dominate an entire field of law for half a century. Llewellyn's success in at least setting the UCC on its initial jurisprudential path may have been the best accomplishment possible.

This article tells a story of accomplishment and loss. Karl Llewellyn achieved great success in implementing his ideas in the UCC. Yet, as nearly half a century has passed, the UCC has undergone substantial revision. The changes have altered not just the substance of the law, but also its underlying jurisprudence. Much of Llewellyn's influence has dwindled as the drafters of subsequent revisions have rejected or ignored Llewellyn's insights from Legal Realism.

This development might have saddened Llewellyn, but it probably would not have surprised him. In his last book, *Jurisprudence*,

Llewellyn observed that two legal styles have competed with each other throughout the history of the nation. In the 1830s and 1840s, judges adopted a rather flexible manner of interpreting the law. Between 1885 and 1910, however, a formal style supplanted this mode of judging. Starting in the 1920s and 1930s, the less formal approach re-emerged, leading to the jurisprudence of the UCC two decades later. Llewellyn, I am sure, could foresee that times again would change, and that the formal approach would regain adherents.

Llewellyn's fading imprint on the jurisprudence of the UCC should influence the law's future interpretation and revision. Article 1 presently contains sections that explicitly instruct courts to engage in purposive interpretation, to rely on supplemental general principles, and to use remedies to compensate aggrieved parties. As the nature of the UCC has changed, these sections have become inconsistent with the rest of the code.

The latest draft of the proposed revision to Article 1 restates Llewellyn's principles in several sections as though the rest of the UCC has not undergone any transformation. The drafters should rethink this decision because the sections no longer reflect the current character of the code. To reaffirm them after so much of the UCC has changed has no justification. Unless the revisers plan to reinvigorate Llewellyn's ideas throughout all of the articles, they should redraft or eliminate Article 1 provisions that misleadingly would state abandoned objectives as general principles.

Discussion Question: Take a look at the Byzantine detail in Revised Article 9 (which is more than twice as detailed as its predecessor) and also look at the complexities of Revised Articles 3 and 4, and then re-examine the Code's statement of purpose in 1-102(2). Do you agree with Maggs that the Code is sacrificing its open-ended flexibility and its focus on *standards* in favor of closed-end *rules* that are not designed to change over time? In particular, look at the first paragraph in Official Comment 1 to Section 1-102, which says that the Code is designed to allow the law to develop in light of new practices among merchants. Do you agree with Maggs that the general statements in Article 1 are increasingly outdated with respect to recent amendments to the Code?

Chapter Five

Interpretation

Judges and lawyers have long struggled to interpret the Code, largely because of its dense language and its unorthodox use of ordinary terms (such as 'perfection') in specialized ways. When construing a Code provision, courts often look to the Official Comments for guidance, yet the Comments are neither law nor legislative history in the proper sense; indeed, many of the Official Comments were written *after* the text had already been adopted. Adding to the confusion, the text of the Code does not make reference to the Comments.

The first two selections in this chapter deal with the question of reliance on the Official Comments. In the first selection, Robert Skilton nicely explains the history of the Comments, ultimately concluding that they perform an essential function by guiding readers through the Code, although he acknowledges that some comments are much better than others. In the second selection, Soia Metschikoff provides a colorful account of why the text of the Code does not refer to the Comments. Finally, Julian McDonnell proposes a methodology for interpreting the Code which he calls "purposive interpretation," and he provides a seemingly plausible series of steps to be followed when construing a Code provision.

Some Comments on The Comments to The Uniform Commercial Code
Robert H. Skilton[1]

The official text of the UCC, as promulgated by the American Law Institute and the National Conference of Commissioners on Uniform State Laws, is accompanied by "comments." In quantity of words, these comments are a great deal more than the text. That says a lot, for the text itself is of no small length.

---

1. Robert Skilton, Some Comments on the Comments to the Uniform Commercial Code, 1966 Wis. L. Rev. 597 (1966). Copyright 1966 by The Board of Regents of the University of Wisconsin System; Reprinted by permission of the Wisconsin Law Review.

It may cause a wry smile that an act intended to "simplify" and "clarify" the law governing important kinds of commercial transactions should be thought to require so much in the way of text and comments. It seems that "clarity" and "simplicity" are here the foes of brevity.

A cynic would opine that the lengthiness of commentary shows that the text does not speak for itself. On the other hand, one impressed with the fundamental fact of life's infinite variety may feel pessimistic about the ability of any text and comments, no matter how lengthy, to supply more than a certain number of answers to some of the myriad situations that the future may have in store. Detail in formations may be good up to a certain point, but after a while the point of diminishing returns is reached. And if the formulator pushes on beyond that point, adding detail, in pitiful hope that he is promoting certainty, he may come to another point—where no one else knows what point he is making.

But considering the large number and the great detail of the sections of the Code's text, the comments, with some few exceptions, cannot properly be charged with being too long. In fact, in a fair number of cases they are exasperatingly short and should have been considerably longer.

As one reads the comments, the question comes, almost sua sponte, what weight should be assigned to them in construing the text?...The [present version of the General Comment by the NCCUSL and the ALI preceeding the text of the Code] says:

> Uniformity throughout American jurisdictions is one of the main objectives of this Code; and that objective cannot be obtained without substantial uniformity of construction. To aid in uniform construction this Comment and those which follow the text of each section set forth the purpose of various provisions of this Act to promote uniformity, to aid in viewing the Act as an integrated whole, and to safeguard against misconstruction.

Referring to this comment, one writer observes: "Perhaps we face here an engineering problem: How high can the comments lift themselves by their own bootstraps?"

His question springs from the fact that the official *text* of the Code has no provision which expressly authorizes or approves use of the comments or gives any special dignity to them. The text is silent. Such reticence contrasts with the 1952 version of the Code. Section 1-102(3)(f) of the 1952 Code had declared: "The Comments of the National Conference of Commissioners on Uniform State Laws and the American Law Institute may be consulted in the construction and application of this Act but if text and comment conflict, text controls...."

Deletion of this subsection came in consequence of the numerous 1956 Recommendations of the Editorial Board for the Uniform Commercial Code, which led to substantial revision of the Code. (The Report of the New York Law Revision Commission, with its analytical background studies of the 1952 text of the Code, had much to do with the 1956 Recommendations.) The reason officially *stated* in the 1956 Recommendations for deletion of section 1-102(3)(f) was that "the old comments were clearly out of date and it was not known when the new ones could be prepared."

Since then, revised comments have been issued, but no blessing on the comments has been reincorporated into the text. So, with no help from the text, the current comments try to "lift themselves by their own bootstraps" [Note to Readers: Recall that only the Code text is enacted as law, while the comments are not enacted along with the text; therefore, in most states there is no Code provision telling courts how much weight to assign to the comments]...

A particular reason for making use of the comments is that they may be viewed as part of the legislative history of the Code. This view gives the comments a special dignity. A more general reason is that they express opinions on meaning and purpose of text and were written by men who supposedly either participated in the drafting of the sections involved or were close to those who did. For the most part these men, in the language of Dickens in *A Christmas Carol*, "prefer to remain anonymous." A still more general reason is that they form a treatise on the Code, and may be consulted as any other treatise, standing on its own merits.

In commenting on the significance of the comments, Professor Honnold observes:

> Embarrassing questions multiply if one subjects the Comments to the standards often imposed for recourse to legislative history. In some states, the revised Comments had not yet been drafted at the time of the Code adoption. In

others it is highly doubtful that the Comments were laid before the legislators in the form of a committee report explaining the legislation which the legislators were asked to adopt.

It would be very wrong, however, to conclude that the Comments are without value to lawyers and to courts. Professor Williston's treatise on Sales has been given heavy weight by courts in construing the Uniform Sales Act on the ground that it reflected the intent of the draftsman [namely Williston himself], although it was written subsequent to the drafting of the Act; courts have repeatedly quoted the Comments in construing the Code.

Surely the Comments may be given at least as much weight as an able article or treatise construing the Code. It is equally clear that the Comments do not approach the weight of legislation; if the statutory provisions adopted by the legislature contradict or fail to support the Comments, the Comments must be rejected.

The point is significant, for we shall see instances, easily understood in the light of the Comments' bulk and the many successive revisions of the Code, where the Comments contradict the statute. More frequent are instances of enthusiastic discussion of significant problems on which the statute is silent.

A thorough job construing the Code calls for using the comments to make sure one has found the pertinent language of the statute, as a double-check on a tentative construction, and as a secondary aid where the language of the statute is ambiguous. However, the editor warns his students that he sternly rejects any reference to Comments until after the pertinent statutory language has been carefully examined in the light of the statutory definitions and the statutory structure. Nuances concerning the precise weight which may be given to the Comments must await further litigation testing the issue.

Each section of the Code has its own section comment. The organization structure of the section comment has four or five subtopics. Under the heading "Prior Uniform Statutory Provision," the first task assigned to a section comment is to cite any provision of the Uniform

Sales Act, the Uniform Negotiable Instruments Act, etc., which covered the same area as the Code section. If a prior uniform act provision is cited, the next comment heading is "Changes." Here is stated in briefest fashion the general nature of the difference between the original act and the Code section. The body of the comment follows. If "Changes" have been indicated (and it is predictable that whenever a provision of an original act is involved, it has been changed in some respect), the body of the comment is entitled "Purposes of Changes" or perhaps "Purposes of Changes and New Matter." If on the other hand no prior uniform provision has been cited, the body of the comment is headed "Purposes." The comment concludes with "Cross References" and "Definitional Cross References," in which citations of other Code provisions bearing on the subject of the section text and comments may be found as well as citations of other Code sections defining terms used.

The "Cross References" and "Definitional Cross References" at the end of the section comments improve the chances that a Code section will be considered in context with due regard to its proper place in the whole. The cross references may be intended to be complete, so as to lead to all other sections which have relationship to the text of the section, or may be concerned only with certain points developed in the section comments. In any event, a person using the Code should not depend upon these citations as exhaustive...

A comment may be (1) expository—seeking to describe the meaning and application of a section of the Code and its relationship with other sections, (2) gap-filling—seeking to suggest answers to questions not precisely covered by the text, or (3) promotional and argumentative—seeking to "sell" a controversial section. And so forth. These classifications are not mutually exclusive...

I do not propose to give a critique or "book review' of the comments considered in their entirety. The very thought is tiring. Suffice to note that the superficial structural uniformity of the comments is not accompanied by qualitative and stylistic evenness. Section by Section, article by article, the comments vary from fullness to practically nothing, from penetration to banality. Perhaps different comment writers had different conceptions of a proper comment. Some comments are probably closer to incorporating research study notes prepared in connection with drafting than others; some comments are merely terse summaries. As to many, the master, Time Deadline, may have had something to do. The comments to one article may on the whole be much better than the comments to another article...

[Skilton then proceeds to analyze situations where the Official Comments are misleading, or where they change the plain meaning of the text. Contemporary examples might include the following: 2-615 provides that a *seller* may be excused from performing a contract due to failure of presupposed conditions, but Official Comment 9 extends this right to *buyers* in certain instances. Section 2-314 creates an implied warranty of merchantability that ostensibly does not apply to sales by non-merchants, yet Official Comment 3 imposes liability on non-merchants for failure to disclose hidden defects in items that they sell. Finally, compare the text of Section 2-201 to its Official Comment and you will find that the Comment mentions the requirement of a quantity term to satisfy the statute of frauds, yet the text does not set forth this requirement].

These rambling reflections are not intended to deny the merit of much of what is said in the comments. Study of the comments is indispensable to a knowledge of the Code.

The writer acknowledges a great debt to the comments. Many times they have given him insight into the meaning of sections. Their presence is comforting—the points they treat and the cross references which follow reinforce understanding.

Perhaps the most difficulty question of all confronting one who seeks answers under the UCC is: Have I hit upon all provisions of the Code which relate to the question at issue, and have I properly evaluated all of them? It would be false and dangerous to assume that the comments (and the cross references) can furnish a *complete* check list. But they help if used with care.

As aids toward understanding and uniform application of the Code, courts may be expected to pay very serious attention to what the comments have to say. We should realize, however, that the comments are the work of human beings—gifted human beings, to be sure, but still human beings.

Discussion Question: Skilton points out that the 1952 version of the Code contained an express provision permitting courts to make use of the Comments in construing the text, and instructing courts that the text should control over the Comments if a conflict arises. This provision was removed in subsequent drafts. Do you think that the

Code should be silent on the Comments (as is now the case under the current version of the Code), or should the Code say something expressly about the Comments, and if so, what should the Code say?

Brief Comments on the Comments
Soia Mentschikoff[2]

At one time the rules on the construction of the Code were much greater in number. One of the things said in the Code [in the actual text itself] was that the Comments—the joint comments of the NC-CUSL and the ALI—could be resorted to by the courts to ascertain the underlying reasons and policies of particular sections and the Code as a whole. That went out for two reasons, both of which are interesting. The first was that some states don't have documentation in the way of legislative history as a bill goes through the state legislature and so do not permit their courts to consult what was happening in the legislature, or the documentation that was before a legislative committee or the legislature, as part of the history of the statute for purposes of construction. This would not have been a sufficient reason [to remove the section of the Code which authorized courts to consult the Official Comments] because, of course, the proposed Code language was an authorizing subsection and would simply change the practice of that state. The thing that really took the proposal out of the Code was Judge Learned Hand who, when the controversy was being explained to the Council of the ALI, looked up over those bushy eyebrows of his and said, "How silly can we get, and how silly can they get? It doesn't matter at all whether it's in or out; of course we'll consult them [the Comments] anyway"; and it was on the statement that the courts would consult them anyway, whether they were officially in or not, that the reference to the Comments went out. This as it turned out was an important step because there had been criticism of the Comments [from the New York Law Revision Commission] and all of this criticism became irrelevant, obviously, once there was no official statement that they had to be consulted by the courts. The courts can do what they like.

Discussion Question: Mentschikoff takes the attitude that courts will consult the Official Comments no matter what, so it doesn't matter

---

2. Soia Mentschikoff, Commercial Transactions: Cases and Materials (Boston: Little, Brown, 1970).

whether the text of the Code expressly authorizes them to do so. Perhaps she underestimates the legitimating effect of having the Code affirm the value of looking to the Comments when interpreting the text. If the text of the Code authorized courts to look at the Comments, wouldn't this lead to increased uniformity, since the courts would anchor their interpretation of a provision with respect to the specific purposes and policies set forth in the Comments?

Purposive Interpretation Of The Uniform Commercial Code
Julian B. McDonnell[3]

Professor Karl Llewellyn and his colleagues fashioned themselves jurisprudes. In significant respects they produced a Code structured by the orientations of the jurisprudential movement known as American legal realism.

Central to the realist movement was a belief in the *necessity* for a "purposive interpretation" of legal institutions. The theory of purposive interpretation is rooted in the concept of law as a means to selected social ends—a method of social engineering. It seeks to define legal standards in terms of the purposes they are designed to implement. It denies that either statutory provisions or common law doctrines can be adequately understood by reference to a standard of ordinary or plain usage. Thus, the realists never tired of resurrecting Justice Holmes' famous declaration: "A word is not a crystal, transparent and unchanged; it is the skein of a living thought and may vary greatly in color and content according to the circumstances and the term in which it is used."

Of course, the realists did not invent the practice of construing language in light of purpose. Such an approach was recognized in Anglo-American law at least as early as *Heydon's Case* in which statutory interpretation was said to demand inquiry into the "mischief and defect for which the common law did not provide" and the "true reason" of the remedy which Parliament had adopted "to cure the disease of the commonwealth." The realists' program was distinguished by the programmatic and unrestrained manner in which they sought to institutionalize this approach.

---

3. Julian B. McDonnell, Purposive Interpretation of the Uniform Commercial Code: Some Implications for Jurisprudence, 126 U. Pa. L. Rev. 795 (1978). Copyright 1978 by the University of Pennsylvania Law Review. Reprinted by permission.

In drafting the Uniform Commercial Code they first delineated central "underlying purposes and policies" of the project as a whole. There are contained in section 1-102(2):

> Underlying purposes and policies of this Act are:
>
> (a) to simplify; clarify and modernize the law governing commercial transactions;
>
> (b) to permit the continued expansion of commercial practices through custom, usage and agreement of the parties;
>
> (c) to make uniform the law among the various jurisdictions.

These goals were not casually derived. They reflect the fact that the drafters thought of the Code as remedial legislation. The Code was drawn to avoid the complexity, obsolescence, and divergent interpretations which had plagued prior uniform laws in the commercial field. In an effort to assure that these objectives were not treated as a mere preamble, the drafters directed: "This Act shall be liberally construed and applied to promote its underlying purposes and policies."

Second, and more particularly, the drafters sought to articulate the policy embodied in each provision of the Code. In so doing they acted more like judges justifying a decision than legislators declaring law by fiat. They defended this approach to drafting as necessary for the attainment of the Code's underlying remedial objectives. Thus, the Chief Reporter listed as his first principle of drafting technique: "The principle of the *patent reason:* Every provision should show its reason on its face. Every body of provisions should display on their face their organizing principle." Llewellyn explained this principle in terms of the demands of rationality and the central objectives of a uniform and adaptive commercial law:

> The rationale of this is that construction and application are intellectually impossible except with reference to *some* reason and theory of purpose and organization. Borderline, doubtful, or uncontemplated cases are inevitable. Reasonably uniform interpretation by judges of different schooling, learning and skill is tremendously furthered if the reason which guides application of the same language is the *same* reason in all cases. A patent reason, moreover, tremendously decreases the leeway open to the skillful advocate for persuasive distortion or misapplication of the

language; it requires that any contention, to be successfully persuasive, must make some kind of sense *in terms of* the reason; it provides a real stimulus toward, though not an assurance of, corrective growth rather than straitjacketing of the Code by way of case law.

Because an objective is usually indicated in a statute itself in but a terse or suggestive manner, the drafters provided a fuller delineation of purpose in the Official Comments to individual Code sections. Although it has not been frequently noticed, the textual portion of the Comments is headed "Purposes" or "Purposes of Change." These express statements of purpose follow citations to prior uniform statutory provisions. The reader is invited to compare a particular Code provision with these earlier texts in order to understand better its remedial function.

The drafters' attempt to use the commentary to facilitate purposive construction was linked with the underlying goal of uniformity. As stated in the introductory Comment to the Code:

> Uniformity throughout American jurisdictions is one of the main objectives of this Code; and that objective cannot be obtained without substantial uniformity of construction. To aid in uniform construction these Comments set forth the purpose of various provision of this Act to promote uniformity, to aid in viewing the Act as an integrated whole, and to safeguard against misconstruction.

A similar theme is evident in the Official Comment to section 1-102 which states:

> The Act should be construed in accordance with its underlying purposes and policies. The text of each section should be read in the light of the purpose and policy of the rule or principle in question, as also of the Act as a whole, and the application of the language should be construed narrowly or broadly, as the case may be, in conformity with the purposes and policies involved.

The unrestrained impetus of purpose is dramatized by the suggestions in the same Comment that courts implement "a statutory policy with liberal and useful remedies not provided in the statutory text," and disregard "a statutory limitation of remedy where the reason of the limitation does not apply." The official commentary indicates that, at least at times, articulated purpose is to control statutory text in Code interpretation.

As drafting the Code gave the realists a unique opportunity to legislate purposive interpretation, so experience under the Code now provides a basis for evaluating this distinctive approach. The considerable body of decisions that construe the Code include opinions unequivocally embracing purposive interpretation and others totally disregarding it...

Issues that appear simple have generated considerable controversy under the Uniform Commercial Code. Consider the widely discussion question: "Is a farmer a 'merchant' for purposes of Article 2 of the Code?" [McDonnell then explains that while the text of the Code is silent on this point, some courts have refused to look at the purposes and policies of the Code in fashioning an answer to this question, instead resorting to dictionary definitions of 'merchant' and 'farmer.' McDonnell then provides a multi-step approach to this question, beginning with the definition of 'merchant' in 2-104, then passing to the purposes articulated in the Comments to the section, then looking at prior drafts of the Code to determine what the drafters were trying to accomplish when they inserted the present definition of "merchant." Ultimately he hits upon Llewellyn's comment that in doubtful and borderline cases, merchant-status depends on a party's level of sophistication. He concludes that the question at hand, 'Are farmers to be considered merchants under the Code?,' cannot be answered in the yes/no fashion that courts have been using, instead requiring a factual determination in each case. He then discusses several other situations where courts have reach inconsistent conclusions by refusing to look at the purposes and policies underlying the Code and opting instead for simplistic solutions].

Part of this Article has been devoted to showing how the methodology of purposive interpretation has either been disregarded or used in the construction of the UCC. Examples were given illustrating how courts [avoid purposive interpretation] to effectuate their own policies in opposition to those of the Code drafters. In contrast to these methods of surreptitious judicial legislation, the method of purposive interpretation was outlined, involving the following steps:

1. Start with the statutory language and read it all as it stands with an eye to the underlying purpose or purposes and the relationship between them.

2. Look for articulation of purpose in the Official Comments.

3. Explore how the present statutory text varies from earlier drafts of the Code and from the treatment of the same subject in pre-Code law.

4. After considering statutory language, Official Comments, and historic context, in *seriatum*, examine these factors in combination for a coherent interpretation.

Purposive interpretation is not a license to be casual with the language chosen by the legislature. It recognizes instead that legislating is a complex and specialized act of speaking that cannot be analogized to the simple command of parent to child. Democratic values according priority to the legislature as the primary policy-making body are more likely to be effectuated if legislative pronouncements are read in a way which takes into account the linguistic problems faced by draftsmen.

Discussion Question: McDonnell's four-step program (actually three steps with a fourth step of stirring everything together) seems intuitively plausible, but complications soon arise. First, how will a court know when it needs to pass beyond the text of the Code to the Official Comments, and then beyond the Comments to prior drafts of the Code? And how much weight should be given to case law (not to mention out-of-state decisions) interpreting the provision in question? Is it plausible for the four-step process to be undertaken in every case, and how will a court know when it has reached the "coherent interpretation" sought in step four? Does McDonnell's four-step process seem less plausible the more you think about it, or do you find it workable?

Chapter Six

Federalization

We saw in Chapter One that the Code project received an impetus from the failure to enact a Federal Sales Act during the late 1930s; this failure suggested to the Code drafters that uniformity should be sought through adoption by all fifty states of a uniform statute. By and large, the Code project has been a success, yet there remains a nagging problem of non-uniform amendments by various states, as well as the problem of convincing all of the states to keep current in enacting the latest versions of the Code. Because of these problems inherent in the use of state law to regulate commercial transactions, the idea of a federal code for commercial law has never quite gone away. The readings in this chapter explore the potential advantages and disadvantages of federalizing the law of commercial transactions. As you already know from reviewing the contents of your statutory supplement, there already exists a high level of federal regulation over commercial transactions in the form of specialized statutes which pre-empt various provisions of the Code. The selections in this chapter address the more radical option of enacting the entire Code (or a similar statute) wholecloth into federal law.

In the first selection, Professors Cohen and Zaretsky nicely explain the advantages and disadvantages of a federal version of the Code, concluding that a better option is to maintain the existing Code while reforming the amendment process. In the second selection, E. Hunter Taylor looks at the problem raised by non-uniform versions of the Code in the various states, and he assesses some proffered solutions, including the interesting possibility of a hybrid federal-state regulation of commercial transactions. Ultimately, Taylor argues that federalization might be the best option, and he sees no insurmountable Constitutional problem with having the federal government regulate commercial transactions. In the final selection, Fred Miller points out some of the dangers of federalization, including the poor track record of Congress in enacting successful commercial laws, and the inevitability of interest-group influence on the legislators who would be charged with drafting the federal Code.

A Modest Solution?
Neil B. Cohen and Barry L. Zaretsky[1]

Comparing the current uniform law process to a hypothetical process of national enactment of commercial law is useful in identifying problems with the current process. Although federal commercial law exists, it is generally limited in scope and is typically not the result of any evaluation of broad commercial policy issues. Consequently, there is no obvious federal experience to use as a guide for comparison.

Nonetheless, let us imagine a new national commercial law—the National Commercial Code (NCC). First, Congress would enact the NCC, which would essentially consist of the current UCC, minus conflict-of-law provisions currently needed to resolve conflicts between different state versions. (It could also create a national filing system to replace state and local filing under Article 9.)

In this hypothetical scenario, perhaps new commercial legislation under the NCC would be drafted under the auspices of a commission appointed by Congress. The commission might retain a reporter and designate a drafting committee and additional advisors as needed. The draft proposals could, if approved by the commission, then be sent to the relevant congressional committees, which could be expected to examine closely the policy choices, but (hopefully) defer to the commission on the "drafting" issues. Unlike state legislatures, these committees would likely have—or have available to them—the resources and expertise to thoroughly consider the policy determinations inherent in the draft.

Congress could also establish a commission to oversee operation and development of the NCC. Congress could give this commission the authority to promulgate rules consistent with the NCC to cover situations not clearly addressed by the text of the NCC. The commission might also, from time to time, issue reports and recommendations to Congress about the operation of the NCC and the need, if any, for amendments. Thus, this commission could be similar to the current Permanent Editorial Board, except that its products, unlike

---

1. Neil B. Cohen and Barry L. Zaretsky, Drafting Commercial Law for the New Millenium, 26 Loy. L.A. L. Rev. 551 (1993). Reprinted courtesy of Loyola of Los Angeles Law Review. Copyright 1993 by the Loyola of Los Angeles Law Review. All rights reserved.

current PEB Commentaries, would carry the force of the law [Note to Readers: the PEB is a collection of law professors and practitioners who represent the NCCUSL and the ALI in an ongoing effort to establish uniformity under the Code. The PEB was formed in 1961 in an agreement between the NCCUSL and the ALI, and it has actively rendered opinions on conflicts and inconsistencies in the Code, thereby providing a single authoritative interpretation for courts to follow in hard cases, such as instances where two provisions seem to be in conflict. In many sections of the Code (such as Section 1-203), reference to the applicable PEB commentary is inserted into the Official Comment following the provision. Your statutory supplement will contain several PEB commentaries, which may become relevant throughout the semester].

Would this hypothetical model represent an improvement over the current UCC process? That certain advantages would exist is undeniable. For example, commercial law would be uniform—a result that has eluded the NCCUSL and ALI ever since the initial promulgation of the UCC. Of course, the cost of this uniformity would be centralized federal control of the rules governing commercial transactions, an area traditionally governed by state law.

Is centralized federal control itself problematic? As a nation, we appear to have moved beyond states' rights slogans to accept broad federal power over matters once considered local. Nonetheless, state regulation of commercial matters has a long, and generally favorable, history in the United States, and a proposal to nationalize commercial law should not be embraced perfunctorily.

Another advantage of nationalizing the commercial law process would be that minor errors could be corrected more easily. Because such errors will always be with us, it is no criticism of the current drafting process to observe that glitches occasionally occur. Yet, just as Congress frequently passes a technical corrections act after major changes in the Internal Revenue Code, errors or ambiguities detected in a new or revised article of the NCC could be quickly and painlessly corrected or clarified after enactment. Under the current process, correction is difficult because each of the fifty state legislatures must act on enactments.

In addition, it would be easier to update the NCC in light of new developments. Because only one legislature need act, it would be possible to revisit regularly the NCC as new issues arise. Consequently, there would be no need to rely on post hoc "official" commentaries and comments to respond to such developments.

Of course, the relative ease with which federal law can be amended is itself problematic. As we have seen with the Bankruptcy Code, interest groups can and do lobby Congress for the passage of special interest legislation that is often inconsistent with the statute's underlying policies. Although interest groups can be, and often are, represented in the current UCC drafting process, they tend to assert less overtly self-interested influence over the policy choices than seems to occur in the federal legislative process. Moreover, once a proposed article is promulgated, whatever influence interest groups normally have with state legislatures is usually reduced to veto power because state legislatures generally are not inclined to deviate from the promulgated uniform text in support of an alternative proposed by an interest group.

On the other hand, although interest groups may have greater influence under a federal model, that model may also be more democratic in terms of providing representation to a broader array of interests. Although recent UCC drafting committees seem genuinely interested in obtaining input from a wide range of interests, the success of that endeavor is unclear. Some groups seem so oriented to the traditional legislative process that, despite an opportunity to participate in the UCC drafting process, they do not become seriously interested in a proposed statute until it reaches the legislature. At that point, under the current UCC process, it is too late to have any real influence. Still other groups are oriented to proposing statutes to resolve identified problems rather than to participate in the drafting of a broad-based statute to avoid problems. In general, because many interest groups pay more attention to federal lawmaking, it is more likely that such groups concerned about commercial issues will take notice of a federal process.

Moreover, commentators have argued that some interests, such as those of consumers, get short shrift from the current UCC drafting process. Even when consumer groups express their views before a drafting committee, the ultimate decisions are often made by a group of commercial lawyers who may not be fully sensitive to consumer issues. Furthermore, the process of drafting a statute that will apply to the entire range of possible transactions, from small consumer transactions to multimillion-dollar business transactions, inevitably leads drafters to pay greater attention to getting the larger transactions "right." From this, it is only a short step to deciding that issues unique to consumer transactions ought to be dealt with in separate, local consumer legislation (which, of course, may never be drafted or enacted). In a federal legislative model, however, such policy decisions are ultimately made by legislators who may be more likely to value the strong interest that consumers have in commercial legislation.

In addition, the process by which policy choices are made under a federal system would likely differ significantly from the process under the current system. Under the current drafting process, it is the understandable desire of the participants to operate by consensus whenever possible. After all, it is unlikely that a provision supported unanimously (or nearly unanimously) by the drafters will later be proven "wrong." On the other hand, this desire for consensus has the serious side effect of creating difficulty in making hard choices. It often results in a statute that avoids hard issues rather than confronts them. By their nature, hard choices are not likely to be made by consensus. While Congress, as an institution, is hardly a hotbed of political courage, it consists of politicians accustomed to resolving many matters by contested votes rather than by consensus. The NCC, therefore, might be more likely to address difficult policy issues. Having a democratically elected Congress debate and decide these issues is likely to bring different results than leaving the issues to the courts.

Federalization of commercial law would also make it easier to harmonize commercial law with other federal concerns. Harmonization has been awkward, at best, under the UCC. For example, Congress was dissatisfied with the provisions in old Article 4 concerning the timing of a customer's right to withdraw deposits from an account. The result of this congressional dissatisfaction was the Expedited Funds Availability Act and its accompanying Regulation CC, which largely superseded Article 4 via the Supremacy Clause. Revised Article 4 sidesteps funds availability issues, leaving banks, customers and their attorneys to deal with a crazy quilt of state law, federal law and federal regulation.

The interaction of the UCC and federal bankruptcy law provides another example of the need for coordination between commercial law and applicable federal law. Although Congress made an attempt in drafting the Bankruptcy Code to harmonize it with the UCC, it is nearly impossible for the UCC to respond in kind. Thus, for example, there are "four-month rules" in the UCC that are derived from the four-month preference period in the old Bankruptcy Act, which was repealed in 1978. It will have taken the UCC at least fifteen years to recognize the shorter ninety-day preference period in the Bankruptcy Code.

The UCC and Bankruptcy Code provide still another example of the need for coordination in the provisions concerning reclamation. The provisions in the UCC and the Bankruptcy Code are similar, but sufficiently different, to create unnecessary interpretive difficulties. Federalization of commercial law would enable Congress to create a single reclamation right that would be effective under the same standards, regardless of whether the buyer commences a bankruptcy proceeding.

Despite the potential advantages of a federal process described above, it is unclear that such a process would be preferable to the current uniform law process. For one thing, the current process, whatever its flaws, is not as susceptible as Congress to blowing with the wind of temporary political fashion. The uniform law drafting process occurs largely out of the public limelight, insulated from many political pressures. While the product of that process must enter the legislative process, it is less likely to be adulterated in that process. It is simply more difficult for a mood or an interest group to capture fifty state legislatures that it is to exert similar influence on one Congress.

Furthermore, although we have hypothesized the existence of a commission that would draft and monitor commercial law, Gresham's law would likely operate to eliminate the advantages of that system. Under the current system, the "best and the brightest" draft a statute that is widely circulated and painstakingly reviewed by both the NCCUSL and ALI for correct policy and for quality of technical draftsmanship. Under a federal system, the inevitable side effect of greater congressional involvement in policy making would be less emphasis on the draftsmanship of the integrated whole. This, in turn, would make it more difficult to attract the high-quality drafters to which we are accustomed. Moreover, a federal statute would, by its nature, be more susceptible to piecemeal revision by Congress. Consequently, there is a significant risk that even an initially well-drafted statute would eventually fall prey to internal inconsistencies and other incoherences that are largely avoided under the current system.

In this respect, the Bankruptcy Code provides a useful example. In the early 1970s, a "blue ribbon" commission evaluated the bankruptcy law, issued a comprehensive report, and proposed a draft bankruptcy statute. Five years after that proposal, Congress enacted a Bankruptcy Code that differed significantly from the proposal. Even the Bankruptcy Code as enacted was the subject of intense lobbying, resulting in a plethora of special interest amendments over the years. The statutory language has increasingly come to resemble the more opaque portions of the Internal Revenue Code, with exceptions to exceptions and paragraph-long sentences. The result today is a far cry from the comparative neutrality of the results of the uniform law process.

Should the current uniform law system be replaced? If future products of the current process prove to be controversial or fall short of the universal acclaim that greeted the initially adopted versions of the UCC, there may well be pressure to move to a different system. Perhaps the best solution to the problems in the present commercial law drafting process is to reform the process, rather than replace it, striving to retain its many virtues while minimizing its structural vulnerabilities...One improvement, apparently already implemented, is to more widely publicize and open the policy-making and drafting process in order to obtain the widest possible range of views. Another improvement may be to pause for a period of time between promulgation of an "official" text and the introduction of that text in the state legislatures; this period could then be used for commentators not involved in the drafting process to ferret out any problems in the text.

A reformed process, improved with these changes and others, could retain the structural virtues of the current uniform law process and produce a better product. So improved, the uniform law process would be even more attractive, reducing pressures to utilize federal legislation or other alternative drafting processes.

Discussion Question: Cohen and Zaretsky provide a wonderfully clear and balanced account of the strengths and weaknesses of federalization versus the current regime of state-by-state enactment. But their analysis is so even-handed that both approaches (state law versus federal law) seem to hold unique benefits and burdens, to the point where a choice becomes difficult. Is there any way to decide which route is superior? Explain whether federalization or the current system appeals to you, and why?

Uniformity and State-by-State Enactment: Contradictions
E. Hunter Taylor[2]

The drafting and state-by-state enactment of the Uniform Commercial Code was heralded as a major milestone, if not the ultimate solution, in the movement to make uniform the commercial laws of the United States. It has proven, in most respects, to be an excellently drafted statute. Yet, the Code, while producing more uniformity than existed previously, is proving incapable of effecting the degree of harmony needed between the commercial laws of the various states.

Both the text and the silences of the Code contain important seeds of nonuniformity. Some significant matters were simply not provided for, thereby leaving the various states to reach their solutions. Other Code sections are worded in such a way as to delegate to each state the choice of which, as between competing interpretations, it wishes to embrace. Drafting mishaps contribute to nonuniformity. The unnecessary incompleteness in the formulation of legal rules and the inadvertent adoption of vague, ambiguous and competing rules produce inconsistent results in like cases.

Even with the most complete and consistent drafting possible, however, and even with a total absence of choice delegation, uniformity is improbable through the process of state-by-state enactment. State-by-state enactment is an invitation to local amendments because it gives each state legislature an opportunity to deviate from the "uniform" act. Unfortunately, the states have been unable to resist this tempting invitation to amend. Thus, by the time the various states enacted the Code it ceased to be uniform. Local amendments are, however, only the first phase in the breakdown of uniformity. One kind of consequence of state-by-state enactment is that the courts of each state have primary responsibility for the interpretation of that state's code. Interpretational mishaps and legitimate interpretational differences are inescapable. With this legion of final arbiters, multiformity it inevitable.

Attainment of more substantial uniformity in commercial law will require significant federal participation in the effort and the accompanying abandonment of the state-by-state enactment model. The de-

---

2. E. Hunter Taylor, Uniformity of Commercial Law and State-by-State Enactment: A Confluence of Contradictions, 39 Hastings L. J. 337 (1978). Reprinted by permission.

gree of federal participation might be as little as federal enactment of a commercial code with major jurisdiction over its application vested in the state courts. On the other hand, it could be in the form of a federal code with jurisdiction over it vested in the federal judiciary. Various interfusions of these models are possible and the choice of the most appropriate model depends in large measure on the degree of uniformity that is sought. While opinions may differ as to the optimum degree of commercial law uniformity, prolonged Balkanization of commercial law is the certain consequences of continuing down the present path of state-by-state enactment.

Some of the more significant categories of diversity producing factors in the Code will be illustrated in this Article by examples from statutory language in Article 2 and from case decisions interpreting Article 2...

The drafters, in the general statement of purpose of the Code, call for the liberal construction and application of the Act, "to make uniform the law among the various jurisdictions." Yet total uniformity on matters of significance was doomed at the outset by the drafters themselves. A blatant example of almost direct sanctioning of nonuniformity on a point of substantial importance is found in section 2-318 on third-party beneficiaries of warranties in the area of product liability.

Under pre-Code law the issue of warranty and privity was in a state of chaos. The confusion existed at two levels. The first concerned vertical privity from whom in the vertical chain of distribution, other than the buyer's immediate seller, did warranties run to the buyer? Some jurisdictions held that warranty protection ran from remote sellers such as manufacturers and wholesalers to the ultimate buyer. Other jurisdictions held that lack of privity prevented recovery by the buyer back against any party other than the immediate seller. Still other jurisdictions continued to recognize privity as a requisite in warranty actions, but utilized fictions to allow the buyer to recover against remote sellers. A few jurisdictions were beginning to replace traditional warranty reasoning with strict tort liability theory, under which neither privity nor disclaimers were relevant.

The second level of confusion, as to which the same degree of discord obtained, concerned horizontal privity: to whom apart from the immediate buyer did the seller's warranty liability run? The traditional view was that the seller was not liable to anyone with whom he had no contractual relationship. Other courts utilized fictions to circumvent the privity requirement in this context.

Against this background of confusion, the drafters were totally silent on the important matter of vertical privity and took a most cautious position on the issue of horizontal privity:

> A seller's warranty whether express or implied extends to any natural person who is in the family of or household of his buyer or who is a guest in his home if it is reasonable to expect that such person may use, consume or be affected by the goods and who is injured in person by breach of the warranty.

Official Comment 3 explains:

> This section expressly includes as beneficiaries with its provisions the family, house, and guests of the purchaser. *Beyond this, the section is neutral and is not intended to enlarge or restrict the developing case law on whether the seller's warranties, given to the buyer who resells, extend to other persons in the distributive chain.*

Left basically undisturbed, pre-Code lack of uniformity on warranty matters continued.

In 1966 the Permanent Editorial Board added the two current additional alternative versions of section 2-318. The first new alternative extends the seller's warranty liability "to any natural person who may reasonably be expected to use, consume, or be affected by the goods and who is injured in person by breach of the warranty." The second alternative is even less restricted. It deletes the "natural person" limitation and the requirement of personal injury, thereby extending the coverage to business entities and allowing recovery for property loss. Some states have now adopted their own version of section 2-318. Most jurisdictions have dropped the vertical privity requirement for recovery in warranty; the requirement still remains in a few jurisdictions. To further exacerbate the differences, a substantial number of jurisdictions have simply replaced the warranty theory with strict tort liability as the primary method for solving problems of product liability. Even within the strict tort liability jurisdictions, the scope of the liability often differs. Thus, Article 2 has not only not produced uniform products liability principles among the various states, but it may also have encouraged fruition of the discord which was present in prior case law...

When a committee engages in drafting a comprehensive piece of legislation, some slips of the pen are inevitable. Such drafting mishaps in the Uniform Commercial Code are of two general types. In some instances there is simply an unnecessary lack of precision which invites nonuniform interpretation. In other instances there is an apparent lack of consistency which creates competing interpretational possibilities.

One prime example of unnecessarily imprecise drafting is section 2-102, which declares the scope of Article 2: "Unless the context otherwise requires, this Article applies to transactions in goods..." In addition, most Article 2 sections are formulated to be applicable to sales or contracts for sale. Thus, so long as a transaction involves nothing more than a sales of goods, Article 2 is clearly applicable. Yet frequently sale of goods transactions have additional dimensions. For example, services may be an integral part of the contract. Article 2 offers no real help in determining to which hybrid transactions it ought to be applied, and several differences in approach have already developed...

Despite its pre-Code failures, the uniformity movement persisted in using the state-by-state approach to the enactment of the Uniform Commercial Code and has continued to reject the one step approach—federal legislation. Several factors have contributed to this choice. First, during a major portion of the uniformity movement, Congress was dominated by rural interests which naturally were mistrusted by commercial interests. Second, Congress' track record with complicated commercial statutes had been something less than awe inspiring. Third, considerable doubt has existed concerning the constitutionality of a federal commercial code. This doubt stems in part from a fourth factor, the deep-rooted, antifederalist, states' rights philosophy which produced the Tenth Amendment. Influenced by territorial instincts and a self-identity need, the states' rights philosophy nurtures the concept that each state is unique and important unto itself. This provincial chauvinism, while related to constitutional doubt, is an important separate factor influencing choice of state-by-state enactment over federal legislation.

Because of the perceived uniqueness of each state, uniformity, while sought, can never be totally attained. The accommodation of the states' rights attitude requires that an overall scheme of harmony in accord with the uniqueness of each state must be the goal. Thus local amendments are inevitable, and there is a need to emphasize, or at least to be free to emphasize, local interests in the application of legal principles. A fifth consideration in the continuing vitality of the states' rights philosophy is the perception that the states' rights philosophy is more consonant with individual liberty and is thus a buffer against the threat of tyranny inherent in a large central government. Those embracing this view fear that federal intrusion into state commercial law could only be a step on the path to overall federal domination of the states. Sixth, the state-by-state approach is said to provide the necessary flexibility for experimentation by one state that could produce a better means for treating a particular type of problem for all the states.

Apart from the philosophical sacrifice of states' rights interests by enactment of a federal commercial code, the Tenth Amendment itself would probably not prevent the constitutional enactment of such a code under Congress' broad commerce power. . . . If Congress can regulate intrastate crimes that affect interstate commerce, certainly Congress can regular intrastate commercial transactions which inescapably must affect the sum total of national commerce . . .

As is almost always the case with any legal goal, uniformity of commercial law can be pursued in a number of different ways. The choice of which is intricately interwoven with difficult value judgments balancing between conflicting themes. Varying degrees of either uniformity or individual state power must be sacrificed depending upon the approach selected.

One approach is a federal commercial code. Of course, such a code would not need to go beyond those matters in which uniformity is perceived as essential. Thus, it could leave substantial leeway for the enactment of supplementary local rules. One method of maximizing uniformity of the essentials of commercial law would be to limit jurisdiction in cases arising under the federal code to the federal courts. Such a drastic shift of state power to the federal government would be politically unattainable, perhaps philosophically unwise, and in any event practically unfeasible because of the effect it would have on the already overcrowded federal courts.

A more practical variation of the federal enactment model would be adoption of the sort of judicial jurisdictional division contained in the Magnuson-Moss Warranty Act. There jurisdiction over actions arising under a federal statute is vested in both state and federal courts. However, the jurisdiction of the federal courts is severely restricted by a substantial jurisdictional amount requirement.

On first blush such approach might seem insufficient to accomplish the desired degree of uniformity because it would still leave the courts of the various states to interpret the code. This approach, however, would preclude local amendments on the essentials of commercial law, and because the Code would not have to be sold on a state-by-state basis, it is likely that more precise drafting could be accomplished on some of the more controversial matters. Thus several important factors contributing currently to nonuniformity would be precluded simply by the enactment of a federal code. Unquestionably, some nonuniformity would be produced through varying interpretations by state courts. Yet, even the interpretationally inspired nonuniformity might well be less than it is today if a federal code were enacted. Professor Grant Gilmore has noted an important outgrowth of *Swift v. Tyson*, in which the Supreme Court held that federal courts would apply the general law of commerce rather than state law in general commercial law cases:

> During the second half of the nineteenth century the Supreme Court of the United States became a great commercial court: the rules which it announced were, in nine cases out of ten, gladly followed by the state courts as well as, of course, by the lower federal courts. A remarkable degree of national uniformity in the law applicable to commercial transactions was in fact achieved over a remarkably long period of time.

If a federal code rather than state law becomes the primary source of our commercial law, it is not at all unlikely that state courts would give considerable deference to federal court decisions.

Of course, as long as no ultimate arbiter of interpretational differences, some differences are inevitable. As long as the various state supreme courts have the final word in a vast majority of commercial cases some variations of the interpretation of a federal code will be inescapable. Perhaps the number of such variations that would pertain under this approach would be negligible.

On the other hand, if an even higher degree of uniformity is thought desirable, there would seem to be a way to accomplish it, and still leave the great bulk of commercial litigation in the state courts. While Congress has never vested general appellate jurisdiction over state courts in any federal court other than the Supreme Court, the language of Article III suggests that there would be no constitutional problem with such a measure. Such an approach, of course, could not guarantee uniformity from circuit to circuit, but certainly the potential degree of nonuniformity possible under such a scheme is considerably lessened. Furthermore, with the availability of *certoriari* jurisdiction from the Court of Appeals to the United States Supreme Court, vital questions upon which nonuniformity between circuits had developed could be resolved by the Supreme Court.

What has happened with the Uniform Commercial Code, when considered along with the history of earlier uniform statutes, suggests that we are again moving toward significant nonuniformity. Because of state-option, alternative sections and local amendments, the Code originated with nonuniformity, and the subsequent decisional process has evolved more and more nonuniformity, to the point of the very multiformity that necessitated the two previous uniformity movements.

Perhaps this is the best possible course. Because of this Code's inevitable breakdown, it guarantees another reexamination and reformulation of commercial law. Each old code will periodically be replaced by a new streamlined uniform code. State-by-state enactment satisfies the needs of the states' rights theme. While it does not accomplish uniformity, it does achieve a degree, though an ever diminishing degree, of basic harmony...

Still, persuasive arguments can be made in favor of a federally-enacted commercial code. Although leeway could be allowed for state enactment of ancillary principles covering matters of local interest, the text of the basic commercial code would be one throughout the nation, making commercial law more readily known and more predictable for business interests. Multi-state business would certainly prefer to use one form and confront only one body of law. Theoretically, a federal code should be a benefit to commerce, which in turn should contribute to overall commercial prosperity. The federal approach would also fulfill the psychological need for symmetry, which is certainly as strong as some of the psychological needs inherent in the states' rights theme. In addition, a federal code would represent recognition of the fact that in a vast majority of commercial cases the "reasonable expectations" of a citizen of one American state are the same as those of a citizen of another state. This, of course, is increasingly the case, given the steady and dramatic rise in the mobility of our citizenry. Finally, a federal code seems to be an idea with history on its side. Though private law remains to a substantial extent a bastion of the states, the trend of this century in American legal history has been toward more and more centralization. As Professor Lawrence Friedman so aptly put it: "Internally, this has been an age of central, national power. The relative strength of the states has melted away; the federal government has grown to a giant size. The federal Caesar fed on the meat of social upheaval, the two great wars and the cold war, a vast depression and a technological revolution." Thus it may be that the time for a federal commercial code has arrived.

Discussion Question: What do you think of Taylor's arguments in support of a hybrid model of a federal commercial law that can be enforced in state courts, along the lines of the Magnuson-Moss Act? Is this a workable compromise between federalization and states' rights?

Is There an Alternative to the Code?
Fred H. Miller[3]

"Is the UCC dead, or Alive and Well?" It might seem odd to ask that question about a statute enacted in all fifty states, which has been termed "the most spectacular success story in the history of American law." However, it may be that all is not as well as the record suggests.

First [as of 1993, when the article was published], while the Code is widely enacted, it is less than fully uniform. After twenty years, Vermont still has not updated its version of Article 9. More than a decade after the 1977 amendments to Article 8, two states, Alabama and Vermont, have not yet enacted the amendments. Even current Code efforts are not uniform. Thus, while forty-four jurisdictions have enacted new Article 4A basically without amendment, new Article 2A, five years

---

3. Fred H. Miller, Is Karl's Kode Kaput?, 26 Loy. L.A. L. Rev. 703 (1993). Reprinted courtesy of Loyola of Los Angeles Law Review. Copyright 1993 by the Loyola of Los Angeles Law Review. All rights reserved.

after its promulgation, is law in only thirty-one jurisdictions, four of those still abide by the original version as it read before it was amended in 1990 to accommodate non-official amendments that California and other states enacted when they embarked on a program of non-uniform amendments to the original text. Moreover, even the text of Article 2A, as enacted in the remaining twenty-seven jurisdictions with the official 1990 amendments, is not uniform, principally but not solely because of what may be termed "consumer related" amendments.

The UCC is unique. It is a uniform law enacted in every state and covers a broad range of both simple and complex transactions of tremendous legal, social and economic significance. In addition to its commercial importance, the UCC is one of the best examples of the viability of state government. It demonstrates that the federal system continues to make sense by evidencing that state legislatures, and cooperating groups like the NCCUSL and the ALI, can do a competent, indeed an outstanding job of crafting and updating state law. Nonetheless, one may reasonably ask: Would it not be more rational, especially given the current degree of federal preemption and internationalization, to replace state action with action by Congress?

These are good reasons to conclude that this alternative is not desirable. First, Congress is seldom able to act responsibly, particularly on a matter as broad and complex as commercial law—at least as Congress is presently structured. Members of Congress rarely study, formulate the details of, or draft legislation themselves. Those tasks are largely delegated to their staffs, who serve the members of Congress directly, or work indirectly on the staffs of the various committees. While the staff for the most part is composed of bright and hard working people, they tend to be young, of short tenure and have very limited real experience. Their knowledge of and experience with economics, institutions, the realities of how commerce functions and its legal processes, comes largely from books. As one consequence perhaps, a continuous lack of realistic rules emanate from Congress. For example, many bankers believe the availability times of the Expedited Funds Availability Act are a cause of serious fraud losses for financial institutions. The discretion and detail many federal laws leave to a regulatory agency also shows Congress's lack of detailed grasp of the problems engendered by the legislation. Another example of Congress's inability to competently legislate detail is demonstrated in the Food Security Act [of which it has been said]: "Although even the most pejorative hyperbole is inadequate to fully express what section

1324 [the Food Security Act] deserves, the following is a frail attempt: Section 1324 is internally inconsistent, unintelligible, and unworkable...It is a disaster."

Second, most observers would also acknowledge that special interests significantly shape, and perhaps even corrupt, the congressional lawmaking process. The legislative hearing process often appears more devoted to establishing a record for reelection than to sorting out facts to frame a solid product. This process often produces an amalgamation of independent provisions derived from the proposals of various groups, which are not always synthesized, rather than an integrated, thoughtfully drafted statute.

Third, the congressional process is usually slow as well as imperfect. The problems referenced above may result in stalemate on a given subject. In other cases, they may prolong focus on a subject that prevents action on other subjects.

A final, but no less important reason for questioning the wisdom of encouraging federal legislation, is more philosophical; it is reflected in the Tenth Amendment to the Constitution and the underlying principles upon which the United States was founded.

Discussion Question: Using this reading and the previous readings in this chapter, try to compile a list of reasons in support of (and against) a federal Code. Where do you come down on this issue? Is there a certain sense in which we are stuck with the present arrangement by sheer inertia, simply because we are accustomed to the Code as state law and aren't willing to face the leg work and uncertainty involved in enacting a federal Code?

Chapter Seven

Critiques of the Code: Form and Substance

This chapter brings together various avenues for criticizing the Code. The first selection comes from David Mellinkoff, an expert on legal language. Although the piece is somewhat dated (and therefore makes reference to Code provisions that have been amended), Mellinkoff captures the frustration that students often feel when they are forced to deal with the Code and its unique terminology. Mellinkoff ultimately concludes that the Code is sloppily drafted, with many provisions representing piecemeal compromises that lack any sort of internal logic.

In the second selection, literary critic and law professor Stanley Fish presents a scorching critique of Section 2-202, the parole evidence rule for the sale of goods. Fish argues that the provision does not achieve its stated goal of limiting the evidence which a court may consider, and instead simply allows courts to surreptitiously look to outside material whenever they desire to do so. Fish also makes the almost humorous point that there is something odd about a parole evidence rule that needs to be explained by an Official Comment outside of the rule itself! Fish's analysis raises doubts about whether the Code can fulfill its stated goals of providing certainty, stability, and uniformity.

The third selection, from Professor Martha Ertman, argues for extending the concept of a security agreement beyond the traditional commercial realm into domestic relations. Specifically, Ertman argues that the concept of a security agreement under Article 9 should apply to the interest held by a divorced homemaker who has foregone her own opportunities to facilitate her ex-husband's career. Ertman's article is highly regarded for its creative extension of Code concepts into a seemingly non-commercial setting.

Finally, I have included a selection of my own, setting forth my thoughts on the strictures of commercial law pedagogy, which focuses too heavily on 'Code-crunching' to the exclusion of moral/social/political issues. By way of discussing the purchase of a Ku Klux

Klan knife at a flea market, I suggest that professors and students need to look beyond the Code itself to explore broader questions of commerce and commodification.

The Language of the Uniform Commercial Code
David Mellinkoff[1]

Uniformity, like inbreeding, can produce works of genius or monsters, sometime both. A case in point is the Uniform Commercial Code.

Twenty-five years after the start of the brainstorming and salesmanship that has swept the UCC across the nation and onto the statue books of all but one state, it is now nearly forgotten that uniformity is only one of several avowed purposes of the UCC. Another purpose is to "clarify...the law governing commercial transactions..." Yet when we learn from the Code that *debtor* can mean someone who is not indebted, that gasoline may be a *farm product*, that *identification* of goods "occurs" when goods have been identified, and that you may revoke an *irrevocable credit*, it is pardonable to suspect that clarification has been junked for the illusion of uniformity. A more detailed look at the Code will harden suspicion into conviction: for all its substantive contributions, the UCC is a slipshod job of draftsmanship.

The Code itself is devoid of the uniformity it prescribes for the substance of the law. The language is now clear, now mud; now grammatical, now illiterate; now consistent, now inconsistent, slapdash and slovenly. It wallows in definition that does not define and definition that misleads—definition for the sake of forgotten definition. It includes many ways of saying the same thing, and many ways of saying nothing. The word "reasonable," effective in small doses, has been administered by the bucket, leaving the corpus of the Code reeling in dizzy confusion. And overshadowing all else, even in a gallery of elaborate ugliness, are the ambiguity and vacuity inherent in the determined and needless use of the long, long sentence...

---

1. Reprinted by permission of The Yale Law Journal and William S. Hein Company from The Yale Law Journal, vol. 77, page 185 (1967).

The Definitions

The striving for precision which is a noteworthy characteristic of the language of the law often leads us to define, whether defining is needed or not. Definition gives an appearance of precision that warms the cockles of the draftsman's heart. At one stroke you can say what you mean, give an easy reference tag for later parts of a writing, and provide the basis for clarity, brevity, and consistency. The rewards are so alluring that it is easy to overlook the prime difficulty—the process of defining—and the attendant burden of remembering to follow your own definitions. The UCC has opted for the rewards and blinked at the difficulties. So much in the UCC is labeled "definition" that it is almost irreverent to ask the preliminary question, "Are there really any definitions at all in the UCC?"

Some of the things the UCC calls "definitions" have hardly any meaning—some no meaning at all—because they are circular. They define a word with the same word, or with a variation of the word so close that you return to the starting point almost unscathed by information. Sometimes the circuit is short and easy to trace; sometimes the circuit winds over hill and dale before sneaking back on itself.

One of the shorter circuits strewn through the UCC is rights-remedy. A definition tells you:

> *"Remedy"* means any *remedial right* to which an aggrieved party is entitled with or without resort to a tribunal.

Two paragraphs on, another definition tells you:

> *"Rights"* includes *remedies.*

Just like that; you are now back at *remedy.* And to make sense of both definitions you had best spell out *remedial right,* which as anyone can see means a *right,* including the *remedy,* to a *remedy,* or a *right,* including the *remedy,* for which there is a *remedy,* which means a *remedial right,* unless the context otherwise requires, in which case you can stay overnight.

Some years ago, a smiling paranoiac offered to prove to our class in abnormal psychology that he was the true Christ and that Jesus was an imposter. "It's simple," he said. "I am the Christ because the Christ wouldn't lie to you." The startling swiftness of that circular explanation is rivaled by the UCC on identification:

> In the absence of explicit agreement *identification* occurs...when the contract is made if it is for the sale of goods already existing and *identified*.

That is to say, when you make a contract for the sale of existing goods, identification occurs when identification occurs, unless you explicitly agree that identification does not occur when it occurs. [A similar circularity can be found in 1-204, which allows parties to agree to any "reasonable time" so long as the time is "not manifestly unreasonable"].

[In the following passages, Mellinkoff treats the circularities in old Articles 3 and 4, and while the analysis is outdated because the Articles have been revised, his analysis is reprinted here because it gives vent to the frustration felt by scores of law students].

The very nature of the writing with which the UCC must deal is made similarly obscure by UCC definitions. In Article 3, subject to context, "'[i]*nstrument*' means negotiable instrument." By itself, that would be a very short circuit indeed, except for the fact that another section quickly gives you the requisites for a *negotiable instrument*. So it may be assumed that *instrument* is simply shorthand usage, like calling someone by his first name. If that usage were uniform, there would be fewer difficulties. But after that beginning, the skein of repeated *instruments* and *negotiable instruments* becomes hopelessly tangled.

For example, *draft, check, certificate of deposit* and *note* are defined in Article 3 so as to be *negotiable instruments*. But "as used in other Articles of this Act, and as the context may require...[those expressions]...may refer to *instruments* which are not negotiable within this Article as well as to instruments which are so negotiable." That is only a starter. For one of these other articles—Article 4—adopts the Article 3 definition of *draft, check,* and *certificate of deposit*, (though not *note*, which is left to fly on its own). But in saying that the Article 3 definition applies to Article 4, the reference is to Section 3-104, without specification of subsection—i.e., without saying that the reference is to Section 3-104(2), which makes *negotiable instruments* of *draft, check, certificate of deposit,* or to Section 3-104(3), which says they may be "*instruments* which are not negotiable." As an added fillip, Article 4 defines *item* to mean "any *instrument* for the payment of money even though it is not negotiable but does not include money...," so it is anyone's guess whether Article 4 is speaking of *negotiable instruments* or something else when in the same section it mentions *item* and *check*.

The mud becomes thicker in Article 9, which adopts the Article 3 definitions for *check* and *note*. As with Article 4, the reference is again to Section 3-104, without specification of the negotiable or the non-negotiable subsections. In addition, Article 9 has its own definitions of *instrument*, which means not only "a *negotiable instrument* (defined in Section 3-104)..." but also securities and other miscellany. Whether this *instrument* swallows up the incorporated definitions of *check* and *note*, or whether they are intended (because separately mentioned) to stand on an independent footing, is not readily apparent.

After wandering in the wilderness of the other articles, it is comforting to return to Article 3, where at least almost from the start you are told that *instrument* means *negotiable instrument*, unless of course "the context otherwise requires." You turn then to [former] Section 3-303, "*Taking for Value*," which speaks of a holder taking "the *instrument* for value," "a lien on the *instrument*," "when he takes the *instrument*," but ends with a resounding thwack— "when he gives a *negotiable instrument* for it..." If that doesn't shake your confidence in the sense of an unadorned *instrument*, you must wait until the final, bitter, unannounced passage of this same Article 3, an article devoted to impressing you with the fact that *instrument* means *negotiable instrument*. The last word says:

> This Article applies to any *instrument* whose terms do not preclude transfer and which is otherwise negotiable within this Article but which is not payable to order or to bearer, except that there can be no holder in due course of such an instrument.

Home at last. An *instrument* is an *instrument*, negotiable or not. If you now reexamine the definition of *negotiation* in the light of this last stab at the meaning of *instrument*, you may come to the conclusion that under the language of the UCC you can negotiate an *instrument* that is *not negotiable*, which ought to be the end of the line...

By word of mouth a canard passes among lawyers that a dead man is responsible for all the language ills of the UCC. If Karl Llewellyn had any failing it was not illiteracy, and in any event there is ample evidence that the UCC had not one but scores of draftsmen.

Too many cooks did not improve the broth, but even that is not a sufficient explanation of the tortured phrasing. The Code itself is the best evidence that the language of the Code was the least important consideration.

What the draftsmen intended was to change the law, and then—above everything else—to make it everywhere the same. The 18th century British dictum that "in all mercantile transactions the great object should be certainty" was taken to mean in the context of the American system that what was needed was uniformity. And the path to uniformity was conceived to be the adoption by everyone of the same statutory words, regardless of what those words were, regardless of whether those words might be so ambiguous as to result in a thousand varying interpretations that ultimately achieve the very opposite of uniformity. Accordingly, the managers of the operation set about drafting and re-drafting, patching and revising, bargaining to achieve agreement among lawyers and carriers and businessmen, bankers and brokers and candlestick makers. Each dickered-out section has its own history of travail. Once agreement was reached, the compromise formula became sacrosanct, no matter what the ingredients. This was it. The result was not so much a code as a paste-up memorandum of agreement. Some of the participants in the individual struggles doubtless knew at the moment of accord what the memorandum meant as to their particular little bargain; and so it was sealed with the understanding that it would go into the ultimate master memorandum unchanged.

Discussion Question: Mellinkoff uses wry humor to bolster his claim that the Code is poorly drafted. Yet his article contains a more subtle criticism, namely that the Code is so circular that it does not *explain* the law, meaning that a lawyer must already know the law prior to reading the Code (not to mention the need for looking up cases to see how the Code has been interpreted). Do you agree with his characterization of the Code as a Frankenstein monster (a "paste-up memorandum") accessible only to those persons who were privy to its painful history, but a confusing mess to the rest of us?

The Law Wishes to Have a Formal Existence
Stanley Fish[2]

Consider the formulation found in section 2-202 of the Uniform Commercial Code:

> Terms with respect to which the confirmatory memoranda of the parties agree or which are otherwise set forth in a writing intended by the parties as a final expression of their agreement with respect to such terms as are included therein, may not be contradicted by evidence of any prior agreement or of a contemporaneous oral agreement but may be explained or supplemented
>
> (a) by course of dealing or usage of trade (Section 1-205) or by course of performance (Section 2-208); and
>
> (b) by evidence of consistent additional terms unless the court finds the writing to have been intended also as a complete and exclusive statement of the terms of the agreement.

One could pause at almost any place to bring the troubles lying in wait for would-be users of this section to the surface, beginning perhaps with the juxtaposition of "writing" and "intended," which reproduces the conflict supposedly being adjudicated. (Is the writing to pronounce on its own meaning and completeness or are we to look beyond it to the intentions of the parties?)

Let me focus, however, on the distinction between explaining or supplementing and contradicting or varying. The question is how can you tell whether a disputed piece of evidence is one or the other? And the answer is that you could only tell if the document in relation to which the evidence was to be labeled one or the other declared its own meaning; for only then could you look at "it" and then at the evidence and proclaim the evidence either explanatory or contradictory. But if the meaning and completeness of the document were self-evident (a wonderfully accurate phrase), explanatory evidence would

---

2. Stanley Fish, "The Law Wishes to Have a Formal Existence," in The Fate of Law, eds. Austin Sarat and Thomas Kearns (Ann Arbor: University of Michigan Press, 1991). Reprinted by permission.

be superfluous and the issue would never arise. And on the other hand, if the document's significance and state of integration are not self-evident—if "it" is not complete but must be pieced out in order to become what "it" is—then the relation to "it" of a piece of so-called extrinsic evidence can only be determined after the evidence has been admitted and is no longer extrinsic. Either there is no problem or it can only be solved by recourse to that which is in dispute.

Exactly the same fate awaits the distinction between "consistent additional terms" and additional terms that are inconsistent. "Consistent in relation to what?" is the question; the answer is "consistent in relation to the writing." But if the writing were clear enough to establish its own terms, additional terms would not be needed to explain it (subsection [b], you will remember, is an explanation of "explained or supplemented"), and if additional terms are needed there is not yet anything for them to be consistent or inconsistent with. The underlying point here has to do with the distinction—assumed but never examined in these contexts—between inside and outside, between what the document contains and what is external to it. What becomes clear is that the determination of what is "inside" will always be a function of whatever "outside" has already been assumed. (I use quotation marks to indicate that the distinction is interpretative, not absolute.) As one commentary puts it, "questions concerning the admissibility of parol evidence cannot be resolved without considering the nature and scope of the evidence which is being offered," and "thus the court must go beyond the writing to determine whether the writing should be held to be a final expression of the parties'...agreement."

Nowhere is this more obvious than in the matter of *trade usage*, the first body of knowledge authorized as properly explanatory by the code. Trade usage refers to conventions of meaning routinely employed by members of a trade or industry, and is contrasted to *ordinary usage*, that is, to the meanings words ordinarily have by virtue of their place in the structure of English. The willingness of courts to regard trade usage as legitimately explanatory of contract language seems only a minor concession to the desire of the law to find a public—i.e., objective—linguistic basis, but in fact it is fatal, for it opens up a door that cannot be (and never has been) closed. In a typical trade usage case, one party is given the opportunity to "prove" that the words of an agreement don't mean what they seem to mean because they emerged from a special context, a context defined by the parties' expectations. Thus, for example, in one case it was held that by virtue of trade usage, the shipment term "June-Aug." in an agreement was to be read as excluding delivery in August, and in another case the introduction of trade usage led the court to hold that an order for thirty-six inch steel was satisfied by the delivery of steel measuring thirty-seven inches. But if "June-Aug." can, in certain persuasively established circumstances, be understood to exclude August, and "thirty-six" could mean seventy-five, or, in relation to a code so firmly established that it governed the expectations of the parties, "thirty-six" could mean detonate the atomic bomb.

If this line of reasoning seems to slide down the slippery slope too precipitously, consider the case of *Columbia Nitrogen Corp. v. Royster Co.* [451 F.2d 3 (4th Cir. 1971)]. The two firms had negotiated a contract by which Columbia would purchase from Royster 31,000 tons of phosphate each year for three years, with an option to extend the term. The agreement was marked by "detailed provisions regarding the base price, escalation, minimum tonnage and delivery schedules," but when phosphate prices fell, Columbia ordered and accepted only one-tenth of what was specified. Understandably, Royster sued for breach of contract, and was awarded a judgment of $750,000 in district court. Columbia appealed, contending that, in the fertilizer industry, because of uncertain crop and weather conditions, farming practices, and government agricultural programs, express price and quantity terms in contracts are mere projections to be adjusted according to market factors.

One would think that this argument would fail because it would amount to saying that the contract was not worth the paper it was printed on. If emerging circumstances could always be invoked as controlling, even in the face of carefully negotiated terms, why bother to negotiate? Royster does not make this point directly, but attempts to go the (apparently) narrower route of section 202. After all, even trade usage is inadmissable according to that section if it contradicts, rather than explains, the terms of the agreement, and as one authority observes, "it is hard to imagine a 'trade usage' that contradicts a stated contractual term more directly than did the usage in *Columbia Nitrogen Corporation.*" The court, however, doesn't see it that way. Although the opinion claims to reaffirm "the well established rule that evidence of usage of trade...should be excluded whenever it cannot be reasonably construed as consistent with the terms of the contract," the reaffirmation undoes itself; for by making the threshold of admissibility the production of a "reasonable construal" rather than an obvious inconsistency (as in 31,000 is inconsistent with 3,100), the court more or less admits that what is required to satisfy the section is not a demonstration of formal congruity but an exercise of rhetorical skill. As long as one party can tell a story sufficiently overarching so as to allow the terms of the contract and the evidence of trade usage to fit comfortably within its frame, that evidence will be found consistent rather than contradictory. What is and is not a "reasonable construal" will be a function of the persuasiveness of the construer and not of any formal fact that is perspicuous before some act of persuasion has been performed.

The extent to which this court is willing to give scope to the exercise of rhetorical ingenuity is indicated by its final dismissal of the contention by Royster that there is nothing in the contract about adjusting its terms to reflect a declining market. "Just so," says the court, there is nothing in the contract about this and that is why its introduction is not a contradiction or inconsistency. Since "the contract is silent about adjusting prices and quantities . . . it neither permits or prohibits adjustment, and this neutrality provides a fitting occasion for recourse to usage of trade . . . to supplement the contract and explain its terms." Needless to say, as an interpretative strategy this could work to authorize almost anything, and is itself authorized by the first of the official comments on section 202 (and why a section designed supposedly to establish the priority of completely integrated writings is itself in need of commentary is a question almost too obvious to ask). "This section definitely rejects (a) any assumption that because a writing has been worked out which is final on some matters, it is to be taken as including all the matters agreed upon." Or in other words, just because a writing says something doesn't mean that it says everything relevant to the matter; it may be silent on some things, and in relation to those things parol evidence is admissible. But of course, the number of things on which a document (however interpreted) is silent is infinite, and consequently there is no end to the information that can be introduced if it can be linked narratively to a document that now becomes a mere component (albeit a significant one) in a larger contractual context . . .

In short, the parol evidence rule is of more service to the law's wish to have a formal existence than one might think from these examples. The service it provides, however, is not (as is sometimes claimed) the service of safeguarding a formalism already in place, but the weaker (although more exacting) service of laying down the route by which a formalism can be fashioned. I am aware, of course, that this notion of the formal will seem strange to those for whom a formalism is what is "given" as opposed to something that it made. But, in fact, efficacious formalisms—marks and sounds that declare meanings to which all relevant parties attest—are always the product of the forces—desire, will, intentions, circumstances, interpretation—they are meant to hold in check...

[T]he law is continually creating and recreating itself out of the very materials and forces it is obliged, by the very desire to *be* law, to push away. The result is a spectacle that could be described (as the members of the critical legal studies movement tend to do) as farce, but I would describe it differently, as a signal example of the way in which human beings are able to construct the roadway on which they are traveling, even to the extent of "demonstrating" in the course of building it that it was there all the while. The failure of both legal positivists and natural law theorists to find the set of neutral procedures or basic moral principles underlying the law should not be taken to mean that the law is a failure, but rather that it is an amazing kind of success. The history of legal doctrine and its applications is an almost Ovidian history of transformation, under the pressure of enormously complicated social, political, and economic urgencies, a history in which victory—in the shape of keeping going—is always being wrested from what looks like certain defeat, and wrested by means of stratagems that are all the more remarkable because, rather than being hidden, they are almost always fully on display. Not only does the law forge its identity out of the stuff it disdains, it does so in public.

Discussion Question: This is a difficult selection, so don't be discouraged if Fish's message is not immediately clear. Fish seems to be implying that the parole evidence rule (and the law more generally) is something of a hollow ritual. With respect to the Code, everybody pretends that there is something called "The Law" which is understandable by the parties in advance, yet the provisions can be bent in so many directions that the Code *can't* provide rules that are knowable in advance. This is precisely the absurdity of the Code's parole evidence rule, which is supposed to prevent a court from looking at extrinsic evidence, yet it allows evidence of trade usage that contradicts the clear writing of the parties. Do you agree with Fish that we delude ourselves into thinking that commercial law has a "formal existence" when in fact it is inherently malleable according to political and economic pressures?

Commercializing Marriage
Martha M. Ertman[3]

> Com-merce... 1: social intercourse: interchange of ideas, opinions, or sentiments 2: the exchange or buying and selling of commodities on a large scale involving transportation from place to place 3: Sexual Intercourse; syn see Business

The dictionary definition of commerce reveals the close, sometimes synonymous, relationship between finance and romance. This linguistic insight is not news to many homemakers who become indigent, or nearly so, upon divorce, despite their years of helping to provide a significantly higher quality of life for their families than they are able to attain post-divorce. The primary cause of displaced homemaker indigency is simple. The work that homemakers do for their families is not commodified. Despite this clarity regarding the cause of displaced homemaker indigency, the search for tools to alleviate the problem has proven elusive.

The commodification of primary homemakers' marital contributions has generated extensive scholarly dialogue, but few have advocated using commercial law to address the economic problems of displaced homemakers upon divorce. Commercializing marriage makes sense because many of the economic problems divorced women face stem from the under-commodification of their contributions to family wealth, and commercial law is tailored to address these kinds of financial issues (at least more so than family law). Moreover, family law has long been rooted in traditional models of gendered domestic roles that obscure the economic value of homemaking. Thus, the financial nature of displaced homemakers' problems begs for economic solutions such as those provided by commercial law.

---

3. Martha Ertman, Commercializing Marriage: A Proposal for Valuing Women's Work Through Premarital Security Agreements, 77 Tex. L. Rev. 17 (1998). Copyright 1998 by the Texas Law Review Association. Reprinted by permission.

This Article proposes that commercializing marriage might solve some of the financial problems of divorced homemakers. Specifically, I propose the use of security agreements, which I call Premarital Security Agreements ("PSAs") to reveal the debtor/creditor aspects of marriages in which primary homemakers enable primary wage earners to maximize their earning potential. PSAs would protect the primary homemaker's interest in the repayment of her "loan" to her primary wage-earning spouse by granting her a security interest in fifty percent of all marital property, most importantly the primary wage earner's post-divorce income. By commodifying the contributions of homemaking to family wealth, PSAs could alleviate the indigency and near-indigency of many displaced homemakers and also increase respect for homemaking. In addition, because the devaluation of homemaking contributes significantly to women's general economic inequality, PSAs might address the related problem of devalued female work in the market.

A conventional security agreement grants a creditor a security interest in a debtor's property to secure repayment of a loan. In the marital relationship, a PSA would grant the creditor/homemaker a security interest in martial property to secure compensation for services she has performed and her foregone opportunities for market participation. By anticipating future payment for these valuable contributions to family wealth (through sharing the primary wage earner's income until death ends the marriage), the primary homemaker, in effect, extends credit to her spouse.

The credit extended by the primary homemaker would be the value of devoting her primary attention to domestic services. This value can be determined using at least three different calculations: the cost of replacing a homemaker's services with market labor; the lost opportunity costs borne by the homemaker by virtue of devoting her time to homemaking instead of market labor; and econometric models based on economic theory and statistical analysis. While the lost opportunity cost model is popular among some commentators, it also has been criticized by feminists for it focus on costs borne by homemakers and failure to account for the benefits primary wage earners enjoy as a result of traditional gendered divisions of domestic labor. Specifically, primary homemakers make it possible for primary wage earners to achieve "ideal-worker" status through full-time, year-round participation in wage labor—largely unhindered by child care or other domestic responsibilities.

This Article proposes a formula that accounts for both the primary wage earner's gains and the homemaker's losses due to their specialization in wage and domestic labor. The formula calculates the debt in two stages, determining first the amount of an annual payment and then how long those payments should last. The proposed annual payment is thirty percent of the difference between the spouses' incomes at the time of the divorce. The proposed duration of these payments is half the length of the marriage plus the difference between eighteen and the age of the youngest minor child. The total debt is calculated by multiplying the annual payment by the duration [the original text includes a diagram at this juncture].

The thirty percent figure represents the primary homemaker's contributions to family wealth by providing valuable services and foregoing the opportunity to develop her own market potential, and it is based on the assumption that the lower-earning spouse does more of the homemaking labor. The annual payment thus reflects how much a primary homemaker contributed to family wealth in a particular year. The durational factor accounts for the homemaker's long-term contributions to family wealth. The length-of-marriage provision (length of marriage divided by 2) recognizes predivorce homemaking contributions and protects the interest of homemakers divorced after long marriages when the children have grown up and left home (or will do so soon). The second part of the durational calculation (18 minus age of youngest minor child), in contrast, accounts for the post-divorce contributions a primary homemaker makes to the primary wage earner's stream of income. If, for example, a marriage ends after five years and one child, the primary homemaker likely has custody of the child and thus continues to perform parenting services that enable the primary wage earner's status as an ideal worker to continue even after divorce. This value is independent of child support. Unlike child support payments, the debt secured by the PSA represents a reimbursement for the primary caregiver's contributions to the ideal worker's income and other family wealth. Child support payments, in contrast, fulfill a divorced parent's duty to share the expenses of raising a child with his or her ex-spouse.

According to this commercial understanding of marriage, the primary homemaker extends credit in the form of domestic services to the primary wage earner. If the marriage remains intact, the primary homemaker/creditor gets a return on her loan by sharing in the primary wage earner's earnings. However, if the marriage ends, the wage earner's debt goes unpaid, and the homemaker/creditor should be able to collect on the loan just as any other creditor can collect an unpaid debt. The formula proposed here determines the amount of the debt, and the PSA secures the debt, enabling the primary homemaker to use self-help methods such as repossession to obtain repayment. If the primary wage earner's post-divorce income is part of the collateral securing the debt, then the homemaker/creditor could garnish a percentage of that income...

Whether the commercialization of marriage is substantive or procedural, statutory or contractual, PSAs significantly contribute to addressing the problems of displaced homemaker indigency and the general devaluation of women's work.

Commercializing marriage through premarital security agreements has the potential to address two seemingly intractable problems of family law and feminism by commodifying primary homemakers' contributions to family wealth and increasing the value of women's work generally. PSAs make sense because they import a solution from one private realm (the market) and apply it to another private realm (the family) in order to solve an essentially financial problem. Modeled on commercial security agreements, PSAs recognize the debtor-credit elements of the spousal relationship in a traditional marriage, and accordingly grant primary homemakers a security interest in fifty percent of all marital property (including the primary wage earners' post-divorce income). The homemaker extends credit to her primary wage-earning spouse in the form of unremunerated homemaking services and lost opportunity costs that enable the primary wage earner to participate fully as an ideal worker in the labor market. The debt is calculated based on the difference between the spouses' incomes at divorce, the length of the marriage, and the age of any children. PSAs build on other proposals justifying post-divorce income sharing and have the unique potential to win support from diverse ideological approaches.

In particular, PSAs satisfy many concerns of legal economic as well as liberal, cultural, and radical feminist approaches. PSAs serve the legal economic goals of efficiency and deterring opportunism in marriage, and they also serve the cultural feminist goal of increasing the social and economic value of caretaking work. While liberal feminists concerns are likely to arise because of the PSAs' potential to create incentives for women to adopt traditional gender roles in marriage, liberal feminists should appreciate PSAs' parallel potential to create incentives for more equal distribution of homemaking and wage-labor in marriage. Despite the anticipated resistance of radical feminists to PSAs' apparent support for traditional gender roles in marriage, PSAs serve radical feminist interests by transforming the cultural category of economically vulnerable housewife into a powerful market player, the secured creditor. In sum, PSAs may have crossover analytical appeal as a solution to the problems of displaced homemaker indigency and the general devaluation of women's work.

Although no single proposal may satisfy every ideological approach, the objections of each of these approaches can be addressed and largely overcome. Furthermore, even if one or more ideological approach rejects PSAs, PSAs could still serve as a procedural tool for implementing other proposals for post-divorce income sharing, or be included in marital or relationship contracts.

Overall, PSAs have both practical and theoretical benefits. On a practical level, commercializing marriage could significantly diminish the economic hardship of divorce on displaced homemakers and their children. On a theoretical level, PSAs may contribute to the evolving social redefinition of gender, and, in doing so, may alter the current low valuation of women's work. If PSAs achieve these lofty goals, they could change the way society thinks about caretaking work and women's labor in general. Commercializing marriage through PSAs has the potential to alleviate the seemingly intractable problems of displaced homemaker indigency and the devaluation of women's work by importing often-overlooked models from the market to address financial inequities in family law.

Discussion Question: This selection is provocative for suggesting that a concept operative in business transactions (the 'security interest') should be extended to relationships. Does Ertman make a convincing case that our notion of 'commerce' should be expanded to include the 'investment' that women are often expected to make by enabling their husbands to assume ideal-worker status? Why is it not considered a "commercial transaction" when a wife performs labor that enables her husband to work more efficiently as a wage earner while she foregoes the opportunity to enter the public sector herself and earn money?

Is the Code A-Political? Some Lessons from Buying a Klan Knife
Douglas Litowitz

Karl Llewellyn once suggested that the Code would not be controversial because the subject of commercial transactions was "very largely non-political." This sounds somewhat quaint to those of us who have grown accustomed to hearing that 'the personal is political,' i.e., that no realm of human association remains autonomous from political forces. *Contra* Llewellyn, the prevailing attitude toward the Code nowadays is to frankly admit that it is a political document to the extent that it enshrines and enables a particular social ontology, for example by approving a particular adjustment of benefits/burdens to merchants, consumers, and banks. The Code also assumes a political stance (albeit a quietism) by refusing to remedy the inequities that occur in the free market. For example, Article Three of the Code refuses to limit the Holder in Due Course Rule to protect consumers who sign promissory notes, leaving this protection to federal and state regulations. But just as Article 3 (standing alone) can impose significant burdens on consumers, Article Two protects consumers by placing additional burdens on merchant-sellers. By adjusting the rights and remedies of competing social actors in this way, the Code takes political stances to some degree even if it is not directly concerned with matters of immediate political controversy.

This last point is especially important: the Code *seems* neutral on its face even though it cannot avoid taking stances on the economic and social conflicts that get played out in the commercial marketplace. The claim that seemingly neutral laws are inherently political has a venerable intellectual genealogy. Indeed, the permeable boundary between law and politics was a central tenet of the Legal Realist movement with which Llewellyn was associated. And this position became even more firmly established in legal scholarship when the Critical Legal Studies Movement put forth the claim that legal doctrine represents a compromise between competing social and political visions that stand in fundamental contradiction. But even if we concede that the Code represents a political choice in sanctifying one possible balancing of divergent social interests (banks versus customers, merchants versus laymen, lenders versus debtors), the Code avoids overtly political language and has a patina of neutrality.

The seeming neutrality of the Code is secured by the fact that most of the key Articles (including Article 2 on Sales and Article 9 on Secured Transactions) can be applied without regard to the actual goods being sold, leased, or used as collateral. Indeed, the UCC places virtually no overt restrictions on the goods which are subject to the contract (one notable exception being the prohibition in Article 9 on using future wages as collateral).

This indifference as to the actual objects of commerce would seem a reflection of free-market ideology which holds that the law should apply equally whether or not the item is a socially useful commodity. One might say that all goods float with equal specific gravity in the Code—the Code does not care whether one is selling life-preservers or 'flesh-colored Christs that glow in the dark' so long as the sale is not criminal. This indifference toward the subject matter of contracts is reflected in the way that we teach the Code to students, with our endless examples of contracts involving 'widgets' and 'units.' We speak in this way to isolate the law as our immediate focus and to avoid talking about the actual object being sold: after all, it is a class in commercial law, not in objects. However, there is something telling about how we gloss over the actual objects of sale/lease/pledge, and we never talk about the implications of a society fixated with commerce. When we teach the Code, we often avoid taking a stance on the morality of the current marketplace. But should we?

Perhaps by ignoring such questions, we miss the opportunity to discuss the political decisions which shape the internal discourse of commercial law. This was brought home to me recently when, after having taught commercial law for years, I found myself puzzling over the purchase of a Ku Klux Klan knife. From the perspective of the Code, this was a simple and straightforward commercial transaction. Yet there was so much in the experience that pushed beyond the formal text of the Code, to the point where the Code itself seemed incapable of capturing the complexities swirling around this legally unproblematic commercial deal.

* * *

My friend Kim and I went to the flea market to buy some fruit. We were in the shadow of the Capitol building in the old South. We came to a booth where a knife vendor was busily displaying knives to five or six men. I casually walked over to see what the commotion was about, and then I looked down and saw a Ku Klux Klan pocket knife staring back at me. This was the real deal, a folding Klan knife with a big KKK professionally engraved above a detailed picture of a hooded Klansman.

I was speechless, paralyzed. A wave of nausea and shock passed through me, but also an unquestionable fascination. I had seen pictures of the Klan on television, and I live in a place where 'Rebel' flags sometimes outnumber 'Yankee' flags, but this was a weapon that could hurt or even kill—with a message of hatred from a racist organization.

I stood awkward, disbelieving. The flea market was crowded with non-Whites, mostly African-Americans, but also some Asians and Hispanics. Did they know that people were buying and selling Klan knives only yards away from them? Did they care? Did the knife still hold symbolic power for these people, or was it not considered a threat? And what about the knife vendor—was he just trying to make a quick buck, or had I stumbled onto something more sinister?

I wedged between two of the men and picked up the knife. I motioned for Kim to come over, "Do you see this?"

She nodded morosely and walked off. She was a Vietnamese refugee who grew up in the South and probably understood the situation better than I did.

I put down the knife and went after her. I said, "That gives me the creeps."

She looked a little shaken, then said, "I think that guy is in the Klan."

"Do you think he knows I'm a Jew?"

"No, you white people all look alike, they can't tell a Jew from anybody else," she said half-jokingly, although I sensed that she was a little distant and preoccupied.

We walked along, bought some boiled peanuts, and looked around. After about 10 minutes we were ready to go, but I had a confession to make: "I'm still thinking about the knife."

"Me too," she said, "When I was little, the neighbors used to say that they would get the Klan on me, and it always scared me."

That's when it occurred to me that I had three choices: (i) to walk away; (ii) to force a moral confrontation with the vendor and the flea market management; or (iii) to buy the knife. I reflected on these options. Walking away seemed too passive. I could force a confrontation, but then I might get my ass kicked, and if a fight erupted I had little reason to expect support from the management at a flea market where several booths were devoted to the Confederacy. And let's suppose I confronted the vendor and he said that he was merely a dealer in other people's knives and that he doesn't support the Klan personally, then what? So I hit upon buying the knife, for two reasons. First, to put it out of commission, and second, to remind myself that hatred of this kind can still be found so easily.

I walked back to the booth and pretended to muse around even though I cared only about the Klan knife. The proprietor looked to be about fifty, with a white beard, amiable enough, with a business-like demeanor. Finally I spotted the knife, and asked, "How much is this black one?"

He looked briefly at me, and said, "Oh, $25. That's a good knife to own, it's German-made, check it out."

This comment did not inspire confidence in a Jew shopping for a Klan knife! I usually bargain for a better price but in this case I didn't want to be responsible for 'Jew-ing' him down. I put down the money, grabbed the knife, and walked away—the transaction was complete. Not a word had been spoken about the Klan. And in his mind, probably nothing needed to be said.

I put the knife in my pocket and walked back to my car, surveying the law in my head. This was a commercial transaction, all right. What did the UCC have to say? Well, this was a "transaction in goods" subject to Article 2 since the knife was a moveable commodity. And Article 2 covers used goods as well, so this knife was covered. This was clearly a "sale" since I was receiving title to goods for a price. And this man was clearly a "merchant in goods" and I was a "buyer." Offer, acceptance, payment, performance, it was all there. And there was even an express warranty as to the German origin of the knife, and perhaps a warranty of merchantability assuming that it was not disclaimed by his invitation to inspect the knife. I certainly accepted the contract by keeping the knife, and since the knife works, I have no claim for breach. And there you have the law—it permits the sale of Klan knives and even governs the transaction from the formation to the remedy stage. The law, as noted earlier, is neutral with respect to the objects for sale. But I couldn't help feeling that the

*transaction raised ethical, political, and social problems that were ig-
nored by courses that I had taught in commercial law: What objects
should be salable? Should we follow Germany's lead and criminalize
the sale of hate paraphernalia, or does this imposition on free expression replicate the Nazi intolerance that it seeks to eradicate? What
should a person do when confronted with a morally repugnant object? What does it say about our culture that virtually anything can
be turned into a commodity and placed on the market? More deeply,
what does it say about our culture that we are so fixated on private
transactions, accumulation, and credit? These are questions that I
knew were important, but I had never touched upon them in the
classroom.*

*So now I find myself the owner of a Klan knife, and I can't resist
picking it up and holding it every so often. The knife is weathered,
dark in the crevices, and worn from usage. One can only speculate on
the hands through which it has passed, and the thoughts of the men
who held it, who I imagine to be child-like and dangerous, but who
were probably ordinary people that weren't too troubled about carrying the knife. Did they treat it as a novelty, or were they prepared to
use it when push came to shove? And did push ever come to shove?
For better or worse, the knife can't talk to me, and so I am left to
stare at it and imagine its past.*

*I still don't know if I did the right thing in buying the knife, and
sometimes I am ashamed to own it. My goal was to take the knife
out of commission, yet in a small but indirect way I might have facilitated a secondary market in Klan knives. And I don't know whether
I did the right thing in not causing a scene and accosting the vendor
for selling it, although I am certain that he would simply feign igno-
rance or say that he was merely filling a market niche. The predominant feeling in such situations is paralysis and confusion, and one's
inability to respond is part of the effect calculated by those who har-
bor a hatred so deep that it cannot be reasoned away. And so you
fumble around, make a choice, and begin to see yourself differently
than you did before the event.*

*In the final analysis, the knife is small and was probably never used
for physical harm, at least that is what I like to tell myself. But its
corrosive power lies in its symbolism, not in its modest physical
properties. It sends a moribund message of hatred and xenophobia in
a world that is becoming inescapably diverse.*

Incidentally, when I got home and looked at the brand name inside the knife, I saw that it said "Hy. Kaufmann & Sons, Solingen." I know that "Kaufmann" simply means "merchant" in German, but what about the "Hy." which presumably stands for "Hyman," a Jewish name? I made some inquiries in Solingen, but there is no record of this company. It seemed too bizarre to contemplate the possibility that a Jewish-made knife from Germany, modified by the Klan, ended up in my hands.

* * *

My goal in telling this story is to point out that the Code avoids a number of wide-ranging moral questions for the sake of efficiency: it does not tell us what objects can be commoditized and placed on the market, nor does it raise concerns about the character of a society in which virtually everything is for sale or capable of being used as collateral. And therein lies the potential limitation: we become so accustomed to working *within* the labyrinth of the Code that we forget the political decisions that shape the Code, and we rarely stop to consider what the Code says about our society. The Code's version of events is important—it is this 'legal version of events' that binds a court of law. But the Code's story is not the entire story, and sometimes the Code is sterile and one-dimensional. We should remember that while the Code seems non-political on the surface (and this is how it appeared to its principal draftsman), the Code remains bound up with inescapable political choices.

Discussion Question: Did the author make a morally defensible choice in purchasing the Klan knife? In your opinion, should law school courses in commercial law focus on the broader political framework for commercial law, or should professors stick to 'Code-crunching'? Do you agree that the Code can be characterized as "political?"

Chapter Eight

Politics of the Code

The plain language of the Code is neither liberal nor conservative, and indeed the Code is often seen as a non-political document. Still, there is a long-standing suspicion (among law professors and in the bar more generally) that the Code favors conservative, big-business interests. This view was bolstered by the removal of consumer protection language from the Code prior to its initial enactment, and by the fact that consumer groups have played a negligible role in drafting amendments to the Code. On the other hand, there are provisions of the Code that impose extra burdens on businesses, such as the warranty and good faith provisions applicable to merchants in Article 2.

In the first selection in this chapter, a key figure in the Code project from its early stages affirms that the Code is essentially a conservative document, and he chronicles the political compromises that were essential to widespread adoption of the Code. In the second reading, Professor Edward Rubin recounts his experience as a participant in the revision of Articles Three and Four, reaching the conclusion that the amendment process systematically excludes consumers, and arguing that the revised Code reflects the lobbying efforts of large corporate interests. Many of the same themes are raised by Professor Kathleen Patchel, who adds a series of thoughtful suggestions for making the revision process more accessible to all parties affected by the Code.

The Principles Underlying the Drafting of the Uniform Commercial Code
Homer Kripke[1]

In accepting the editor's invitation to write an article on the underlying concepts of the Code I made it clear that I had no intention of writing in the field of jurisprudence. It is my purpose, rather, to ex-

---

1. Homer Kripke, The Principles Underlying the Drafting of the Uniform Commercial Code, 1962 Univ Ill. L. F. 321 (1962). Copyright 1962 by the Board of Trustees of the University of Illinois. Reprinted by permission.

press certain fundamentals resulting from the conditions under which the Code was drafted.

The nature of the Code project was such that only in the faculties of the law schools could the requisite manpower be found to do the drafting. True, dozens of practicing lawyers devoted untold evening hours to reviewing drafts, and participated in two-and-three day committee conferences again and again, as well as attending the twice-a-year joint meetings of the sponsor organizations held over a period of years. But only the law faculties could devote the time in large enough quantities to the enormous task of drafting and redrafting. Only the law faculties had the background of adequate knowledge of the existing uniform acts, where they were obsolescent, and where the interpretations created lack of uniformity. Only the faculties had adequate time for the necessary research.

It must be admitted that if the final outcome of the Code had been left to the drafting staff, the Code would have embodied some changes more striking than those preserved in the final result, because the staff was far more daring than the committees and sections and the general membership of the sponsor organizations. To avoid any possible misconstruction, let me be specific about this. The drafting staff were not radicals—not communists, or anarchists, or revolutionaries of any kind. Rather, their penchant for considering solutions that might seem drastic to the membership of the sponsor organizations arose in part from the vantage point of their scholarship and their teaching positions. They were familiar with the varying solutions to different problems in the several states, and they were free of the convictions of some local practicing lawyers that any particular familiar solution is embedded in the natural order of things. The provincial reaction that a familiar solution is immutable showed itself frequently among the practicing lawyer members in such problems as the comparative rights of chattel lienors and real estate lienors to chattels which become fixtures, or the presence or absence of a filing requirement for retail conditional sale contracts.

The draftsmen were potentially more iconoclastic than their final work product would indicate. Without intending any revolutionary substitutions of strange systems of law and without evidencing a lack of regard for private property and other basic institutions, they were open-minded in the search for clear-cut solutions for some of the difficulties. The abolition of "title" as a solution of problems in the law of sales is one example. The abolition of the distinctions between the different forms of chattel security is another. But similar drastic thinking put forward on a trial balloon basis in other instances did not survive. I can recall, for instance, a discussion among some members of the drafting staff as to whether to Code ought not to cut down the advantage of a lender taking a secured position as against the unsecured position of the trade creditor, and whether the field of credit transactions was not a place for requiring all creditors to be on an equal footing. I do not suggest that the staff would have presented a draft based on so revolutionary a concept even if they had not realized that such a draft would have been unacceptable, but the incident illustrates the readiness of the drafting staff to examine critically the most fundamental assumptions in the search for an appropriate structure of law.

Some part of the staff's suggestions came from a tendency to see problems in terms of the strong against the weak. In particular, they were concerned about protecting the rights of consumers. Thus, the staff wanted to enact a Retail Installment Sales Act within the Code, and they were induced to drop the proposal only by the clear demonstration that uniformity was impossible and that local policy was being determined by local statutes state by state. The staff wanted provisions insuring that consumers would not lose their defenses against third party purchasers of retail installment contracts, a provision embodied in the 1954 Code. When it was ultimately deleted, a provision was inserted preserving any similar principle that might exist as a matter of local law in a particular state. The staff members were concerned with oppression of the consumer time buyer by tie-in clauses which would preclude his ever completing payment for the articles first purchased. To meet this problem they produced an obscure restriction on after-acquired property clauses in financing of consumer goods. They saw the advantage of nonfiling in the case of small consumer conditional sales contracts, but were faced with the problem of the rights of innocent parties. At one point their proposed solution was simple—let the finance companies take the loss, by providing for nonfiling, but protect innocent purchasers. Thus the creditor interests would have been helpless. The solution finally reached is one of the weakest compromises in the Code. It neither provides a clear nonfiling rule not as a practical matter is it protective of the innocent purchaser...

Similar in nature is the fear of the "fine print" in the form contract written by the big fellow, to the prejudice of the little fellow. Forgetting the matter in which industrial giants like the automobile and aircraft companies purchase from numerous small suppliers, the drafting assumes that the seller is the big fellow and the buyer the little fellow. Thus, an exclusion of implied warranties of fitness must be "conspicuous." Many cases dealing with contractual exclusion of warranties are dealt with under the topic of "unconscionability." Contracts to limit certain warranties to the immediate buyer, as distinguished from members of his household, are made unenforceable.

The draftsmen were also much concerned about "unconscionable" contracts. The basic section, 2-302, permits the court to find clauses to have been unconscionable *when made*. But in early versions of the official comments, the staff made this section into one under which the courts had a roving commission to protect against unequal bargaining power or too drastic results in practice. The proposed comments gave meaning to the section far beyond the words as written, and evidenced a quixotic spirit which is fortunately missing from the comments in their final form.

Another feature of the draftsmen's approach was the desire to put the major risk on the professional, or the institutional party...The most conspicuous examples of this tendency are certain rules of risk of loss on the destruction of goods. Who takes the risk of loss? Not the buyer under certain conditions nor the seller under other described conditions, but the professional insurer!

Another such approach, which permeates the article on sales, is embodied in the concept of "merchant." For the man fitting this definition there are numerous special rules imposing higher standards than for other persons. But who is a merchant? Section 2-104(1) defines him in a manner that at first blush seems obvious.

> 'Merchant' means a person who deals in goods of the kind or otherwise by his occupation holds himself out as having knowledge or skill peculiar to the practices or goods involved in the transaction...

Thus a shoe retailer is a merchant in shoes and a coal dealer is a merchant in coal. So much is self-evident. But more may lurk in the definition. Could a lawyer be a merchant in coal and in shoes, because he has knowledge of the "practices...involved in the transaction?" The writer once opposed this definition at a meeting of the Editorial Board, on the ground that the last phrase quoted was a "sleeper," and would make a purchasing agent or a lawyer a merchant in any business, because he would have knowledge of the practice of businessmen in all businesses to read and answer their mail, to accept or reject offers, and the like. The drafting staff made it clear that that was exactly what they intended. I then opposed the definition on the floor at the joint meeting of the sponsor organizations, on the ground that the application of this artificial definition to lawyers, purchasing agents of institutions, and others would unfairly take persons by surprise. Another speaker said that he would support any opposition if the definition had this surprise element, but that the definition could not possibly mean what I suggested as to lawyers. No member of the drafting staff corrected his misapprehension, and the definition was therefore approved by the joint meeting. But the official comment to the definition makes it clear that "banks or even universities, for example, well may be 'merchants'" as to "non-specialized business practices such as answering mail," and a lawyer or a bank president is cited as a person who is not a merchant when not acting "in his mercantile capacity." In this example the extra duty put on the professional may well be reasonable, but I still feel that the method of achieving it through an artificial definition of shifting meaning is dangerous and undesirable...

Whatever may have been the academicians' desire for more thorough-going changes in the law, it was recognized that, in order to be promulgated by the sponsor organizations as their product, the Code had to be conceived as a fundamentally conservative piece of amendatory legislation. The Code was prepared as a joint enterprise of its sponsors, the American Law Institute (whose prior work had been in the field of *Restatement* of the law) and the National Conference of Commissioners on Uniform State Laws (the principal thrust of whose labors had been toward *uniformity*, not radical revamping). The drafts had to be approved by the Joint Editorial Board, by a Section of the National Conference, and by the joint membership meetings of the two organizations. The final product then had to be approved by the House of Delegates at the American Bar Association. While these institutions contain a sprinkling of judges and law school professors, fundamentally their membership is drawn from lawyers who have the interest and the ability to devote time to legal matters beyond the making of a living, i.e., principally the successful partners of established law firms with a corporate or other monied practice. Needless to say, the overall social, economic, and legal bent of such persons is conservative. As was proved with issue after issue on the floor of the joint meetings and in the work of the committees or sections, these lawyers instinctively react in opposition to any fundamental reshaping of the relative strengths of debtor and creditor, of secured creditor and unsecured creditor, of buyer and seller of warehousemen and depositor, of carrier and bailor, or of bank and depositor. While they were willing to rectify matters where the law had developed lack of uniformity, their natural bent was opposed to change where the existing law presented a clear pattern.

A conspicuous example was Article 4 on bank collections. The drafting staff originally sought to put heavy responsibilities on the banks and to limit contractual exoneration from liability. Bank counsel opposed the staff's drafts vigorously. At one point the matter seemed likely to be settled by dropping Article 4 from the Code, but a draft acceptable to bank counsel ultimately became part of the Code.

Not only were conservative tendencies present during the drafting; they were visible on the horizon at the legislative stage. The draftsmen and the members of the sponsor organizations knew that to draft a dead-letter bill would accomplish nothing. The Code had to be enacted. Its very size created problems. The draftsmen had found commercial law to be a seamless web and had decided to produce a commercial *code* instead of a series of revised self-contained uniform acts. Thus, anyone who opposed a part opposed the whole Code. The size of the bill then increased the area for potential opposition. On the other hand, this same size made it unlikely that reasoned presentations to understanding legislators was an available means of defense of the Code against attack. The Code was "lawyers' legislation," largely outside the potential understanding of most members of state legislatures, and too big to be grasped by even the studious lawyer members. Difficult legislation like this without a popular appeal can seldom be passed without a broad consensus of agreement of interested parties. The determined opposition of well-knit groups tends to induce the legislature to do nothing, which is a victory for the opposition. The Code would have been a sitting duck target for any determined special interest or combination of special interests who chose to attack one or more features of the bill persistently. Thus, it was important not to arouse the opposition of banks or finance companies, warehouse companies, railroads, or other private trade groups.

The staff of academicians and the general membership of conservative practicing lawyers thus acted as counterbalances to each other's tendencies. In my opinion the final result gave greater weight to the practicing lawyers than to the staff's viewpoints.

The result is a code that is unquestionably amendatory rather than revolutionary. In sales, the great apparent revolution is the elimination of the title touchstone in the statement of the applicable rules, but this is merely lawyers' technique. The essential law and practice of sales are fundamentally unchanged in the handling of the vast majority of transactions or in the resolution of litigated issues. Similar results are true of the revisions of the other uniform acts. The article on letters of credit is new, but its defenders make the point that it merely restates existing practice. Article 9 looks new and shiny, with a startling new terminology, but it turns out to be primarily a modernization and adaptation of prior legislation in the same field, such as the Uniform Conditional Sales Act, Uniform Trust Receipts Act, Factor's Lien Act, and chattel mortgage statutes.

The present writer states this conclusion as to the Code's pervading conservatism without the slightest intention to impugn the Code as a "sell-out." On the contrary, the result is eminently desirable. There was no demand for a revolutionary reshaping of commercial law, but only for an effort to modernize and to regain uniformity. The result is in keeping with the general nature of the work of the sponsor organizations and with the expectation of the many state legislatures and individual legislators who have approved the Code in reliance on the recommendation of the sponsor organizations and without detailed study.

Discussion Question: Kripke begins the essay by justifying the conservatism of the Code as a *tactical* move for securing enactment, but he ends by suggesting that conservatism was *justified* since there was no generalized demand for reshaping the commercial law. Kripke sees nothing problematic about saying that the Code was the result of compromises (between academicians and practitioners, between consumers and business interests), but how often are we *enthralled* and *inspired* by compromise solutions? Go back to the General Comment preceding the Code and examine the key players in the drafting of the Code (Kripke is listed under Article 9), and then ask yourself whether these people were in a position to forge a fair compromise between the competing interests of consumers and businesses.

Thinking like a Lawyer, Acting like a Lobbyist
Edward L. Rubin[2]

My involvement with the process of drafting the revisions to Articles 3 and 4 began in the spring of 1986, when I was asked to serve as Chair of an American Bar Association subcommittee devoted to this issue. The general committee was the Ad Hoc Committee on Payment Systems, and consisted in its entirety of two subcommittees: mine, devoted to reviewing the Articles 3 and 4 revisions, and the subcommittee on wire transfers, which was devoted to reviewing a proposed new article of the UCC, designated Article 4A. The two subcommittees had an overlapping membership and always met in tandem; the principal distinction between them was the identity of the chair.

I had not been involved with the drafting process in any way before being asked to serve on the subcommittee. My participation was limited to a role typical of legal academics: writing a long, rather complicated article about the subject matter under consideration. This article, coauthored with my colleague, Robert Cooter, applied economic analysis to the problem of loss allocation in payment law, and concluded that this law, particularly the UCC, should be more protective of consumers. It helped me get tenure, but I have no vivid recollection of its having persuaded anyone. Consequently, I was flattered to be asked to serve as an ABA chair—even the chair of a subsection of an ad hoc committee—and it is with a twinge of regret that I now realize, for reasons to be described below, that the ABA will never ask me to chair anything again...

We met three or four times a year, from June of 1986 through August of 1990, after which I resigned my position as chair for reasons to be described below. Invariably, one meeting was held at the ABA's annual convention, which takes place in early August, and another was held at the annual meeting of the ABA's Business Law Section, in March or April. One or two other meetings unconnected with general ABA events were also held at various locations around the country. These later meetings typically lasted two full days, with one day

---

2. Edward L. Rubin, Thinking Like a Lawyer, Acting Like a Lobbyist: Some Notes on the Process of Revising UCC Articles 3 and 4, 26 Loy. L.A. L. Rev. 743 (1993). Reprinted courtesy of Loyola of Los Angeles Law Review. Copyright 1993 by the Loyola of Los Angeles Law Review. All rights reserved.

devoted to my subcommittee, and the second devoted to the subcommittee for Article 4A.

In theory, the meetings were open only to members of the Ad Hoc Committee on Payment Systems, but any member of the ABA who was interested in the subject matter could join the committee. The membership list varied from about 60 to 110 people—with one sudden surge to 133, as will be explained below—but attendance at each meeting usually ranged from 20 to 40. Most of these were "regulars" although there were always a few people who emerged off the membership list for a single meeting before vanishing from sight once more. Both the members of the overall committee and the regular attendees at the two subcommittee meetings were predominantly bank attorneys, corporate attorneys who dealt with their firm's cash management operations, attorneys in private firms who represented banks or large corporations, and law professors. In addition, there usually were representatives from the Federal Reserve System, the New York Clearinghouse and the American Bankers Association...

Articles 3 and 4 codify bank practices regarding check collection, as well as existing understandings about promissory notes, but their crucial provisions—the ones that produce almost all the controversy—involve the allocation of losses between banks and their customers. For a long time, commentators on the UCC drafting process have expressed doubts about the ALI and NCCUSL practice of relying on bank lawyers to draft such provisions. The bank lawyers on the ABA committee had heard this criticism of course; when asked about it, they typically declared: "When I participate in an advisory committee, I check my clients at the door." This was true; with the exception of Thomas Baxter, who explicitly and effectively represented the concerns of the Federal Reserve System, none of the attorneys on the committee defended the particular interests of the bank for which they worked, or which retained them. What these attorneys did not check at the door, however, was their conceptual framework. Contemporary philosophers and anthropologists assure us that doing so would be impossible, and even efforts to imagine doing so, like Rawls' *A Theory of Justice*, have been subjected to intense criticism. In any event, the bank attorneys who participated in the ABA committees certainly had their conceptual frameworks in the room with them. Part of this conceptual framework was the product of being white, male and upper-middle class, as virtually all these attorneys were. Indeed, the very image of checking one's clients at the door would occur most readily to someone who frequents restaurants with coat check facilities; I generally wind up at McDonalds, where I try to keep my possessions *really* close to me. Beyond their lack of diversity, the bank attorneys on the committee tended to see the world from the perspective of their clients. To them, banks are reputable, well-run institutions, struggling to make a decent profit in an economy buffeted by recession, a political environment that imposes unnecessarily stringent and detailed regulations and a world of intense, ever-increasing competition. Consumers who make claims against banks, on the other hand, tend to be careless, mistaken or dishonest. They are not bad people, but when they lose money, their natural tendency is to blame the bank, or if they know they were at fault, distort the facts so that the bank will take the loss... Had consumer representatives been in the room, I am certain they would have found the bank attorneys' picture of banks and consumers somewhat fanciful. Consumers, they would have said, are generally honest; fraud losses on checking accounts, for example, are extremely low and virtually all of these losses are attributable to real criminals, not errant consumers. Banks, on the other hand, are rarely solicitous of individual consumers, and they are reluctant to absorb losses or forego profits when the hapless consumer can be made to pay. In addition, they are inefficient, regularly committing errors whose consequences they are unwilling to accept.

There is very little empirical evidence available about these matters, certainly not enough to support or refute either set of images. The bank attorneys' reflexive belief in the trustworthiness of banks and the irresponsibility of customers springs from a characteristic way that lawyers think. Lawyers cathect with their clients. They do not think of themselves as hired guns, mercenaries, trained barracudas or any of the other bellicose figures that their critics depict. Instead, they see themselves as helping people carry out desirable activities or enforce their legal rights. This is true even for general litigators who switch from plaintiff to defendant, buyer to seller, borrower to lender, new entrant to dominant firm with each case, yet always seem to be convinced that the client who walked in the door and retained them should prevail. It is all the more true for corporate attorneys who work within a single industry, or specialized litigators who always represent one side. When that single industry consists of people whose social class and economic status are the same as the attorney's, bonds of friendship will be added to the process of client identification. Over time, these forces generate a conceptual framework, a general orientation toward the world. It is possible for lawyers to check their clients at the door—attorneys in law firms switch clients fairly regularly, and in-house lawyers can always imagine moving to a different company within the industry. What they cannot leave behind them is a set of identifications, beliefs and personal bonds built up over decades of practice. These identifications, beliefs and bonds constitute their career, their sense of themselves as productive members of society, and form a comprehensive framework through which lawyers perceive the issues in their field...

[Rubin then proceeds to discuss some of the issues that raised conflicting interests between banks and their customers, such as the legal standard for when a bank should be liable to a customer for failing to comply with a stop payment order, and the process of 'check truncation,' explained below]. Under existing check collection systems, the check itself traces a commercial circle from the drawer to the payee, to the depositary bank, the intermediary bank, the drawee or payor bank and as a canceled check, back to the drawer. With truncation, the physical check is cut off at some point and its journey is completed by electronic transmission of the information it contains. Simple truncation stops the check at the payor bank, so that the customer receives a statement with a list of charges but no canceled checks. Nothing in the current UCC prevents this practice, but it does not reduce collection costs to any significant extent. Radical truncation stops the check at the depositary bank and transmits nothing but electronic information through the collection process...

In the ABA committee, the task of pointing out the potential difficulties that these provisions would create for ordinary consumers fell largely to the law professors. I recall being particularly vociferous about the subject. We suggested that consumers might be bewildered by a list of numbers, and that a fair truncation system should impose some obligation on the banks to supply consumers with the information they would need by requiring that banks report the name of payees, or provide "carbonized" checks, or use some other mechanism. In addition, we thought that banks should be required to provide a copy of the actual item, or the item itself, within a defined period of time and at a reasonable cost, because a customer's bank had no particular incentive to retrieve the item from some remote location and the consumer would be in a very poor bargaining position at the time of the request. I also thought that a balanced statute should impose a penalty on banks that failed to produce a requested item and that the formula that has proven to be effective in the Truth in Lending Act, a liquidated sum plus attorney's fees, would be appropriate.

Each time these points were raised, most of the other committee members reacted as if a faux pas had been committed. There was a slight rustling of people in their seats and a few sidelong glances; then one of the bank attorneys, with the most subtle suggestion of a sigh, would undertake to explain to me why the suggested changes were unnecessary. In the first place, he would say, truncation is a new idea, and we should not encumber it with rules whose effects cannot be anticipated. Requiring banks to provide the name of the payee would involve massive redesign of the banks' automatic processing equipment and thus delay, if not prevent, the advent of truncation. As for rules and sanctions governing check retrieval, these are entirely unnecessary; banks need customers and have no desire to ignore their legitimate requests. Requiring the payor bank to obtain items within a specified period of time, under threat of civil liability, is unreasonable because that bank would not have control of the check. All that such a requirement would achieve would be to create another impediment to truncated check collection. At the conclusion of this statement, usually delivered in parts by several different people, there was a general nodding of heads and an unspoken air of "let's proceed" . . .

[I]n the ABA Committee, and, as far as I could tell, in the ALI-NC-CUSL Drafting Committee, only two of the three principal interests—financial institutions, corporate users and consumers—were represented. Apart from bank attorneys and corporate attorneys of various sorts, the only significant group consisted of commercial law professors, five or six of whom were regular attendees. They were quite knowledgeable about the law, though no more so than many of the bank and corporate attorneys, but they had very little impact on the overall tone of the meetings. To begin with, they held diverse views, ranging from those who focused on consumer issues to those who strongly supported the revision process. More significantly, however, they seemed to lack authority as far as the other members were concerned because they represented no one other than themselves. The bank attorneys could claim, however subtly, the support of the industry, as well as a superior knowledge of bank operations; the corporate attorneys could speak with the authority of major nonfinancial enterprises. Because both subcommittees usually operated by consensus, rather than by vote, this rendered the influence of the professors even less than their relatively meager numbers would suggest.

The obvious counterweight to all these bank and corporate attorneys would have been some representatives from the consumer movement. As indicated, these representatives could have been expected to express exactly opposite beliefs about the relative trustworthiness of banks and consumers, beliefs based upon their underlying perception of the world. Like the bank attorneys, they would have expressed their views with a relatively high degree of unanimity, and with the political force of their organizations. Their presence might have generated an adversary dynamic leading to a balanced statute, just as the clash between two represented parties in a court of law is expected to produce a just result.

No consumer representatives were part of the Ad Hoc Committee when it was established; however, none were invited, as far as I know, and none volunteered. Fairly early in the course of our meetings, the chair of the committee, Roland Brandel, noted this deficiency and invited Gail Hillebrand of Consumers Union to join. Hillebrand attended several meetings; she spoke out on the stop payment issue and ultimately wrote a strong statement opposing the revisions. But Hillebrand's participation was constrained by a lack of funding and a lack of time. The bank and corporate attorneys generally had their travel and daily living expenses paid by their bank or firm; the law professors were sometimes reimbursed by their institution or in my case, because I was the chair, by the ABA itself. Hillebrand had no funding and thus was able to attend only those meetings held near her home in the San Francisco area. In addition, Consumers Union is understaffed, with only four attorneys in the San Francisco office and only eleven nation-wide. In addition to payment law, Hillebrand had to cover all other UCC topics, the Community Reinvestment Act, home mortgages, unfair debt collection practices, consumer credit, Truth in Lending and abuses involving raw milk. This would have created difficulties if dealing with an ordinary statute; it presented particular difficulties with respect to Articles 3 and 4, which are arcane and technical and which demand, as commercial law professors and their students know, long periods of unrewarding study...

It did not seem appropriate for me to lead the subcommittee when my views diverged so markedly from those of the members, so I resigned my position as chair in November of 1990...

One month later, I was scheduled to go to Sacramento to testify before a committee on the California legislature on a consumer protection bill, when I noted that the Article 3 and 4 revisions were being considered by the Senate Judiciary Committee on the very day I would be there. I quickly sent a letter of opposition to the legislative staff, and appeared before the committee on May 21, 1991. In my testimony, I concentrated on loss allocation issues, but I also addressed NSF checks and check truncation. The committee members were particularly struck by the truncation provisions and the lack of accompanying protection for customers. My impression was that they had no idea what the revisions contained. Apparently, the legislature assumed the bill was good legislation because it was introduced under the auspices of the ALI and the NCCUSL, and was sponsored by one of California's most respected state senators, Robert Beverly. Had I not testified, it probably would have been placed on the "Consent Calendar" and passed without discussion. After being made aware of the potential problem with the bill, however, the Senators tabled it pending further analysis...

Although the ultimate result of my efforts in California were somewhat meager, I had been struck by the initial lack of attention that unopposed bills seem to receive in state legislatures, and I quickly wrote a letter to the legislatures of all the states that had not yet enacted the revisions — so far as I could determine. Most of these letters seem to have been lost, but I tried to keep track of legislative developments in the states and write follow-up letters when the revisions came to the attention of the legislators. My letters produced some results, again because the legislators were apparently unaware of the bill's provisions until a letter of opposition arrived. In Michigan, the bill was withdrawn from the floor of the House of Representatives, after having been passed by the Senate, for further consideration; in Washington State, the House Financial Institutions and Insurance Committee refused to approve the bill without further study. Colorado rejected the revisions, largely through the effort of Neil Littlefield, a professor at the University of Denver, and so did West Virginia, largely through the effort of David McMahon, of West Virginia Legal Services Plan, Inc. In several other states, including New Jersey, New York and Texas, my letter reached study commissions to which the legislature had initially referred the bill. In still others, it vanished or was ignored, and the revisions sailed through the legislature.

Throughout the process, the ALI and NCCUSL adopted the same

stance. If I did not manage to attract the attention of anyone in the legislature, they would simply present the revisions as an uncontested bill. I was never once informed by either organization that the revisions were being introduced or considered in any state. If I did manage to bring consumer concerns to someone's attention, the ALI and NCCUSL would respond with a fairly massive lobbying campaign, often spearheaded by the Bankers Association of the state. Lengthy documents were prepared, representatives of various organizations flew to the state capitol, and individual meetings with state legislators were held. Consumers Union was described as endorsing the revisions, and Hillebrand had to write to several state legislatures explaining her actual position.

Needless to say, I lacked the resources to counterbalance all, or indeed any, of this heavy lobbying artillery. I was unable to travel to any state legislature except Washington's where I happened to have taken a family vacation. I also was unable to keep track of legislation as it moved through the various state legislatures, and I certainly could not lobby individual legislators.

None of this is surprising, of course. ALI and NCCUSL behaved exactly the way any American organization behaves when it is trying to get legislation passed. When they could get their bill through without anyone opposing it, or even noticing it, they took advantage of that opportunity. When they faced opposition, they responded by trying to overwhelm that opposition or by using allies, like the various Bankers Associations, to put political pressure on the legislators. Nor is it surprising that I was unable to respond in kind. Lobbying legislatures is a game played by organizations, and there is no way for an individual to participate unless he is H. Ross Perot.

But the fact that the ALI and NCCUSL played the game like ordinary lobbyists is in itself worth noting. They are, after all, not interested parties but organizations that purport to represent the public interest. They claim legitimacy for their legislative products not only on grounds of expertise, but also on grounds of the democratic process— that their products have been enacted by the various state legislatures. Yet they made no effort to educate the legislators, to acknowledge the disadvantages of their proposals, or to encourage outsiders to participate. Instead, they did what any advocacy group does—they used every legitimate method to ram through the legislation...

In the process of drafting and enacting the revisions of Articles 3 and 4...banks were well represented; corporate users were represented intermittently; but consumers were virtually unrepresented. The result was that the banking industry and its attorneys dominated the entire process, save for a few brief interludes. This dominance was amplified by the fact that the representatives involved were lawyers, with their characteristic tendency to bond with their client group.

The banking industry is entitled to be represented, of course, and it can be expected to lobby assiduously for its positions. But the American Law Institute and the National Conference of Commissioners on Uniform State Laws should not lend their names to the bankers' enterprise. When they do, as occurred with the Article 3 and 4 revisions, they give the banking industry the ability to clothe itself with public policy, and to overwhelm most state legislatures with a false aura of public-oriented impartiality. This was a disgrace. If the ALI and NCCUSL cannot do better under their present structure, both organizations should be extensively reformed or entirely abolished.

Discussion Question: Rubin points out the irony in a situation where the *American* Law Institute and the *National* Conference of Commissioners on Uniform State Laws are working at the behest of banking interests instead of representing individual *Americans*! Do you see any problem with letting the banking and corporate interests assume a leadership role in the drafting and amendment process, given that the lawyers for these interests are well-organized and knowledgeable while the consumer groups are stretched too thin to participate in a meaningful way? Can you think of any method for ensuring that every group affected by the Code gets a voice in the amendment process? Does Rubin's account generate a sense of outrage, or do you see the revision and lobbying process as an instance of 'politics as usual'?

Interest Group Politics, Federalism, and the Uniform Laws Process
Kathleen Patchel[3]

It is always much easier to criticize what exists than to make suggestions for change. For that reason, it seems somewhat unfair to do

---

3. Kathleen Patchel, Interest Group Politics, Federalism, and the Uniform Laws Process: Some Lessons from the Uniform Commercial Code, 78 Minn. L. Rev. 83 (1993). Reprinted by permission.

the former without at least making some preliminary attempt to do the latter. What follows are merely tentative suggestions—as an outsider to the Conference [the NCCUSL], I am not privy to a number of the considerations that necessarily will influence the Conference's decisions about the desirability and feasibility of any given alteration to its present process. Further, every organization has an ethos known only to those familiar with it. Thus, those who are involved with the uniform laws process are in the best position to decide how to address its problems. Nevertheless, several areas for consideration suggest themselves.

A. *Open Up the Drafting Process*

It seems clear that the Conference and, to the extent it becomes involved in this process, the ALI, need to open up the uniform laws process—to make it more visible and accessible to a wider range of interests—at the drafting stage. Adequate representation of all affected interests is critical if the Conference is serious about its goal of drafting the "best" legislation with regard to a given subject matter.

Further, interest group theory suggests that opening the drafting process is going to require affirmative action on the part of the sponsoring organizations to actively seek the participation of consumer representatives. The obstacles consumers face in organizing for collective action, particularly with regard to technical statutes, coupled with the Conference's lack of visibility and accessibility to the general public, indicate that the Code's sponsoring organizations cannot assume that consumer representatives will appear of their own initiative.

The diversity of consumers also suggests that having one consumer representative, while it is better than having none, is not likely to present the full range of consumer views on an issue. Just as the Conference would not consider all business interests affected by the Code to be adequately represented by the appointment of one "business" representative, it must recognize that multiple consumer representatives may be required as well. In addition, just as the Code drafters have actively solicited input from nonlawyers with regard to the concerns of business groups, they also should include nonlawyers with consumer views in the process. The sponsoring organizations also need to take a broader view of when uniform commercial laws affect consumer interests. The drafters cannot remove consumer interests from the Code simply by deciding not to include affirmative consumer protection provisions. Unless the drafters feel comfortable including a provision in the draft of a uniform commercial law that "This Article does not apply to consumer transactions," then consumer interests are involved, and should be provided with adequate representation...

B. *Provide the States with a Basis for Independent Decision*

The sponsoring organizations also need to make the state legislatures more aware of the policy choices that have been made in the course of drafting a uniform law presented to those legislatures for enactment. The drafters of uniform legislation do not view themselves as the proponents of a particular interest. When they make a policy choice it is presumably for reasons other than favoritism to one interest or the other. The choice made, the alternative positions rejected, and the reasons for the decision all need to be clearly articulated for the benefit of the state legislatures. It is not enough to present them with the text of the statute—particularly for complex statutes like Articles 3 and 4, the text of the statute is not likely to make the policy choices that it represents obvious to the average legislator. The comments, at least as currently drafted, are also insufficient. They are not always available, and sometimes not even drafted, at the time a state's legislature is considering a uniform law. Moreover, the comments tend to be technical themselves, as they are designed to guide courts in the appropriate interpretation of the Code rather than to guide legislators in their enactment decision. What is needed is the drafters' detailed explanation of the major policy choices that have been made—and the alternative choices that have been rejected—during the drafting process, set forth in plain language and human terms...

C. *Place the Importance of Enactment in Perspective*

The sponsoring organizations also need to change their attitude about the importance of the enactment of proposed uniform laws as the measure of their success. The history of the Code clearly reveals that the need to gain the support of powerful interest groups that otherwise might block enactment of a uniform law makes the uniform laws process vulnerable to the influence of these groups at the drafting stage. Further, at the enactment stage, the desire to have uniform laws passed quickly and without amendment works against allowing legislatures to give them independent, informed considerations.

Thus, at the drafting stage, the drafters of uniform laws need to be particularly concerned that the need to satisfy business interests with the political power to block a uniform law at the enactment stage does not become the driving force behind the substance of uniform laws. "Consensus" should not be obtained by cutting out the interests of those with opposing views but less political clout. In addition, as discussed above, at the enactment stage, the sponsoring organizations need to be willing to allow the legislatures to determine the merits of the policy choices represented by the uniform legislation for themselves—and, in fact, need to assist them in their ability to do so—even if this creates a greater likelihood that the uniform law will be amended, or not enacted at all...

Nevertheless, if true consensus cannot be reached, the Conference should either abandon the project, or in an appropriate situation, draft the law that it considers to represent the better position, even though adopting the position may cause a politically influential group to oppose the law in the state legislatures. As the Conference itself has recognized, uniform laws can have value apart from their "enactability," through their influence on other state legislation that is enacted, as well as through their impact on case law and teaching practices.

D. *Choose the Appropriate Legislative Forum*

Given the position that the uniform laws process occupies within our federal structure, the sponsoring organizations need to consider when deciding whether to draft a uniform law whether the subject matter of the proposed law is one better dealt with by state rather than federal legislation. The rationale for using the uniform laws process rather than allowing uniformity to occur through federal legislation should be explicitly articulated as part of the decision to undertake a drafting project. A vague reference to states' rights is an insufficient justification—the states never were intended to be the source of law on all subjects. The fact that the area has been addressed through a uniform law in the past should not, of itself, be sufficient either. The changed conditions that have led the sponsoring organizations to conclude that the uniform law must be revised may also indicate in a given situation that such revision should occur through federal legislation. Moreover, given the broadened scope of conflict available at the federal level, the Conference must consider whether the uniform laws process is going to provide an adequate forum for all affected interests to present their views and reach consensus about the substance of the law. If the answer to this question is "no," then the project should not be undertaken...

Consideration of the uniform laws process in light of modern group theory demonstrates that, as currently structured, the process is an inadequate mechanism for drafting commercial legislation designed to reach reasonable accommodation among the interests of all affected groups. Grounded in outmoded notions of group dynamics and the workings of federalism, the current uniform laws process, rather than providing a means for drafting laws that represent neutral, best solutions to commercial law issues, tends instead to produce only solutions that are the most amenable to the business special interests that largely dominate it.

The uniform laws process, at both its drafting and its enactment stage, exacerbates the inherent organizational disadvantages under which consumer interests operate. At the drafting stage, its lack of visibility and accessibility to the general public combined with the absence of any formal structure for obtaining input from all affected groups, means that consumer interests are not likely to receive effective representation. At the enactment stage, the pressures associated with the drive for uniformity in the fifty states discourage independent consideration by the state legislatures of the drafters' policy choices; these pressures thus may deprive the states of the opportunity to make truly informed and autonomous decisions about the appropriateness of those policy choices, and rob the policy choices themselves of the legitimacy that the approval of a democratically elected, politically accountable body otherwise might give them. At the same time, the Conference's largely uncritical acceptance of a states' rights rationale for utilizing the uniform laws process with regard to every issue ignores the considerable impact that process has on the dynamics of federalism, and consequently, on the development of policy at the appropriate representative level.

It is not surprising that a process developed one hundred years ago needs revision. Moreover, revision of the uniform laws process at this point would not be the first time the process has been altered to reflect changing conceptions of decision-making processes. When the Conference was founded in 1892, formalism still was the dominant legal paradigm. In a jurisprudential structure in which legal principles had an independent existence, and thus correct solutions were waiting to be "found" through a process of deductive reasoning, employing a group of experts to find them made good sense.

By the time the Code project came along, however, the Realist movement had largely undermined formalism. Deductive reasoning did not "find" right answers; rather, it merely provided solutions based on the initial premises chosen by the reasoner—the important thing was how one picked the premises. Llewellyn believed that these premises could be discovered in the patterns of commercial practice, and he altered the uniform laws process accordingly to reflect this belief by involving in it those business interests in whose collective practices he thought the appropriate rules of commercial law lay waiting to be found.

Modern jurisprudential concepts, however, have moved beyond the notion that the development of law involves the discovery of pre-existing legal principles, whether found in the abstract through deductive reasoning or in the concrete through ascertainment of commercial practices…Legal rules represent choices from among a number of possible alternatives—choices that involve policy decisions to value some interests more than others. When presented with a law that purports to represent the "best" solution to a given problem, the natural question to be asked is, "Best for whom?"

Modern theories of decision-making are the standards by which the uniform laws will and should be judged, and under those standards it does not, as currently structured, make the grade. It seems the Conference is faced with a choice: it must either alter its process to make it truly representative, or abandon its assertion that the commercial laws it drafts are the "best" solutions for the problems with which they deal. If it does nothing, it runs the risk not only of tarnishing its reputation as a neutral body of experts, but also of becoming a marginal player in the future development of the commercial law.

Discussion Question: Do you agree with Patchel's interesting suggestion that Llewellyn set the tone for over-involvement of business interests in the Code project by virtue of his focus on commercial practices and customs that were best understood by business persons as opposed to consumers and academicians? What do you think about her suggestions for improving the uniform laws process?

Chapter Nine

Commercial Law and Literature

The great bulk of 'legal fiction' involves criminal trials; not surprisingly, much less has been written about commercial disputes. For example, most people are familiar with the fiction of Scott Turow and John Grisham, but they would be hard pressed to name a single author who writes fiction about commercial transactions. Still, this chapter brings together some fictional pieces that will stimulate your thinking about the Code.

In the first selection, the famous Argentine writer Jorge Luis Borges raises the absurd situation where a mapmaker produces a map that is the same size as the territory. For our purposes, this parable raises the question of whether the 'map' offered by the Code and the Official Comments is so detailed that it eclipses the 'territory' of commercial transactions.

The second and third selections deal with the law of sales. First, in a vignette pulled from the underground bestseller *Trainspotting*, Irvine Welsh tells a disgusting story of a waitress who takes revenge on her customers. Then, noted author Thomas Wolfe describes the dark side of a Company devoted to marketing a product to people who don't need it, while trapping the salesmen in a humiliating system of rewards and punishments.

The fourth and fifth selections deal with negotiable instruments. First, A.P. Herbert, who wrote humorous stories about cases in London courtrooms, tells the story of a taxpayer who submits a negotiable cow to the taxing authorities. Then Patrick Combs tells a story about doing something that most of us have wanted to do but were afraid—depositing a junk-mail check of the Publishers Clearinghouse variety.

On Rigor in Science
Jorge Luis Borges[1]

...In that Empire, the Art of Cartography reached such Perfection that the map of one Province alone took up the whole of a City, and

---

1. Jorge Luis Borges, Dreamtigers (Austin: University of Texas Press, 1964).

the map of the empire, the whole of a Province. In time, those Unconscionable Maps did not satisfy and the Colleges of Cartographers set up a Map of the Empire which had the size of the Empire itself and coincided with it point by point. Less Addicted to the Study of Cartography, Succeeding Generations understood that this Widespread Map was Useless and not without Impiety they abandoned it to the Inclemencies of the Sun and of the Winters. In the deserts of the West some mangled Ruins of the Map lasted on, inhabited by Animals and Beggars; in the whole Country there are no other relics of the Disciplines of Geography.

Discussion Question: Is the Code so detailed that it resembles a useless point-for-point map?

Eating Out
Irvine Welsh[2]

Oh god, you can tell; it's just going to be one ay these nights. Ah prefer it when it's busy, but when it's deid like this, time drags. No chance ay tips either. Shite.

There's hardly anybody in the bar. Andy's sitting looking bored, reading the Evening News. Graham's in the kitchen, preparing food that he hopes will be eaten. Ah'm leaning against the bar, feeling really tired. I've got an essay tae hand in the morn, for the philosophy class. It's on morality: whether it's relative or absolute, and in what circumstances, etcetera, etcetera. It depresses me tae think aboot it. Once ah finish this shift ah'll be up all night writing it up. It's too mad.

Four guys come into the restaurant, obviously drunk. Crazy. One looks vaguely familiar. Ah think ah might have seen him at the University.

What can I get you? Andy asks them.

-A couple of bottles of your best piss...and a table for four...he slurs. Ah can tell by their accents, dress, and bearing that they are middle to upper-middle-class English. The city's full of such white-settler types, says she, who's just back from London! You used to get Geordies and Scousers and Brummies and Cockneys at the Uni,

---

2. Irvine Welsh, Trainspotting (New York: W.W. Norton & Co., 1996).

now it's a playground for failed Oxbridge home-counties types, with a few Edinburgh merchant-school punters representing Scotland.

Ah smile at them. Ah must stop having these preconceived notions, and learn to treat people as people...They sit down.

One sais: —What do you call a good-looking girl in Scotland?

Another snaps:—A tourist! They speak very loudly. Cheeky cunts.

One then sais, gesturing in my direction:—I don't know though. I wouldn't kick that one out of bed.

You prick. You fucking doss prick.

Ah'm seething inwardly, trying tae pretend ah didnae hear that remark. Ah cannae afford tae lose this job. Ah need the money. No cash; no Uni, no degree. Ah want the degree. Ah really fucking want it more than anything.

As they study the menu, one ay the guys, a dark-haired skinny wanker wi a long fringe, smiles lecherously at us. —Orlroit dahlin? He says, in a put-on Cockney accent. It's a vogue thing for the rich tae dae on occasion, I understand. God, I want tae tell this creep tae fuck off. Ah dinnae need this shite...aye ah do.

—Give us a smile then, girlie! A fatter guy sais, in a booming officious voice. The voice ay arrogant, ignorant wealth unchallenged, untainted by sensitivity or intellect. Ah try tae smile in a condescending wey, but ma face muscles are frozen. Thank fuck as well.

Taking the order is a nightmare. They are engrossed in conversations aboot careers; commodity brokering, public relations and company law seeming tae be the most popular, in between casually patronising and trying tae humiliate me. The skinny creep actually asks me what time ah finish, and ah ignore him, as the rest make whooping noises and dae a drum roll on the table. Ah complete the order, feeling shattered and debased, and depart tae the kitchen.

Ah'm really shaking wi rage, wondering how long ah can control this, wishing that Louise or Marisa were on tonight, another woman tae talk tae.

—Can't ye get these fuckin arseholes oot ay here? ah snap at Graham.

—It's business. The customer's always right, even if he's a fucking knob-end.

Ah remember Mark telling me aboot the time he worked at the Horse of the Year Show at Wembley, doing catering wi Sick Boy, one summer years ago. He always said the waiters have power; never mess wi a waiter. He's right, of course. It's now time tae use the power.

Ah'm smack-bang in the middle ay a heavy period, and ah'm feeling that scraped out, drained way. Ah go tae the the toilet and change tampons, wrapping the used one, which is saturated wi discharge, intae some toilet paper.

A couple of these rich, imperialist bastards have ordered soup; our trendy tomato and orange. As Graham's busy preparing the main course, ah take the bloodied tampon and lower it, like a tea-bag, intae the first bowl ay soup. Ah then squeeze its manky contents oot wi a fork. A couple ay strands ay black, uteral lining float in the soup, before being dissolved wi a healthy stir.

Ah deliver the two pate' starters and two soups tae the table, making sure that the skinny, gelled fuck-up has got the spiked one. One ay the party, a guy wi a brown beard and phenomenally ugly, protruding teeth, is telling the table, again very loudly, aboot how terrible Hawaii is.

—Too bloody hot. Not that I mind the heat, it's just that it's not like the rich, baking heat of Southern California. This place is so bloody humid, you just sweat like a pig all the time. One is also continually harassed by peasant scum trying to sell you all their ridiculous trinkets.

—More wine! the fat, fair-haired prick perpetually booms at us.

Ah go back tae the lavvy and fill a saucepan with ma urine. Cystitis is a problem for me, particularly during ma periods. Ma urine has the stagnant, cloudy look, which suggests a urinary-track infection.

Ah dilute the carafe ay wine with ma pish; it looks a bit cloudy, but they're so smashed they winnae notice. Ah pour a quarter ay the wine intae the sink, topping up the carafe with ma pish de resistance.

Ah pour some more ay ma pish ontae the fish. It's the same colour and consistency as the sauces which marinate it. Crazy!

These pricks eat and drink everything without even noticing.

It's hard tae shite ontae a piece of newspaper in the toilet; the bog is small, and it's difficult tae squat. Graham's also shouting aboot something. Ah manage a small runny turd, which ah take through and mix up wi some cream intae the liquidiser, and merge the resultant mess wi the chocolate sauce, heating away in a pan. Ah pour it ower the profiteroles. It looks good enough tae eat. Too radge!

Ah feel charged wi a great power, actually enjoying their insults. It's a lot easier tae keep smiling now. The fat bastard has drawn the short straw though; his ice-cream is laced wi ground up traces of rat poison. Ah hope Graham doesn't get intae trouble. I hope they dinnae close the restaurant down.

In my essay, ah now think that ah'd be forced tae put that, in some circumstances, morality is relative. That's if ah was being honest with masel. This is not Dr. Lamont's view though, so ah may stick with absolutes in order tae curry favor and get high marks.

It's all too mad.

Discussion Question: If this was a class in Torts, this selection would be easy to analyze—there is clearly a battery, outrageous conduct, and negligence per se for violating criminal laws. And if this was a class in Contracts, there would clearly be a breach of contract, and the elements would be easy to state. Is the analysis equally simple under the Code, and if not, what does this say about the Code? To answer this question, first answer the scope question—Does the Code apply here (see Section 2-314(1))? Second: What are the terms of the contract? Third: Is there a breach of warranty? Fourth: What are the damages?

The Company
Thomas Wolfe[3]

George considered himself lucky to have the little room over the Shepperton garage. He was also glad that his visit had overlapped that of Mr. David Merrit, and that Mr. Merrit had been allowed to enjoy undisturbed the greater comfort of the Shepperton guest room, for Mr. Merrit had filled him with a pleasant glow at their first meeting. He was a ruddy, plump, well-kept man of forty-five or so, always ready with a joke and immensely agreeable, with pockets bulging with savory cigars which he handed out to people on the slightest

---

3. Thomas Wolfe, You Can't Go Home Again (New York: HarperCollins, 1968). Copyright 1934, 1937, 1938, 1939, 1940 by Maxwell Perkins as executor of the Estate of Thomas Wolfe. Copyrght renewed 1968 by Paul Gitlin. Reprinted by permission of HarperCollins Publishers, Inc.

provocation. Randy had spoken of him as "the Company's man," and, although George did not know what the duties of a "Company's man" were, Mr. Merrit made them seem very pleasant.

George knew, of course, that Mr. Merrit was Randy's boss, and he learned that Mr. Merrit was in the habit of coming to town every two or three months. He would arrive like a benevolent, pink-cheeked Santa Claus, making his jolly little jokes, passing out his fat cigars, putting his arm around people's shoulders, and, in general, making everyone feel good. As he said himself:

"I've got to turn up now and then just to see that the boys are behaving themselves, and not taking in any wooden nickels."

Here he winked at George in such a comical way that all of them had to grin. Then he gave George a big cigar.

His functions seemed to be ambassadorial. He was always taking Randy and the salesmen of the Company out to lunch or dinner, and, save for brief visits to the office, he seemed to spend most of his time inaugurating an era of good feeling and high living. He would go around town and meet everybody, slapping people on the back and calling them by their first names, and for a week after he had left the business men of Libya Hill would still be smoking his cigars. When he came to town he always stayed "out at the house," ane one knew that Margaret would prepare her best meals for him, and that there would be some good drinks. Mr. Merrit supplied the drinks himself, for he always brought along a plentiful store of expensive beverages.

George could see at their first meeting that he was the kind of man who exudes an aura of good fellowship, and that was why it was so pleasant to have Mr. Merrit staying in the house.

Mr. Merrit was not only a nice fellow. He was also "with the Company," and George soon realized that "the Company" was a vital and mysterious force in all their lives. Randy had gone with it as soon as he left college. He had been sent to the main office, up North somewhere, and had been put through a course of training. Then he had come back South and had worked his way up from salesman to district agent—an important member of the sales organization.

"The Company," "district agent," "the sales organization"—mysterious titles all of them, but most comforting. During the week George was in Libya Hill with Randy and Margaret, Mr. Merrit was usually on hand at meal times, and at night he would sit out on the front porch with them and carry on in his jolly way, joking and laughing and giving them all a good time. Sometimes he would talk shop with Randy, telling stories about the Company and about his own experiences in the organization, and before long George began to pick up a pretty good idea of what it was all about.

The Federal Weight, Scales, and Computing Company was a far-flung empire which had a superficial aspect of great complexity, but in its essence it was really beautifully simple. Its heart and soul—indeed, its very life—was its sales organization.

The entire country was divided into districts, and over each district an agent was appointed. This agent, in turn, employed salesmen to cover the various portions of his district. Each district also had an "office man" to attend to any business that might come up while the agent and his salesmen were away, and a "repair man" whose duty it was to overhaul damaged or broken-down machines. Together, these comprised the agency, and the country was so divided that there was, on the average, an agency for every unit of half a million people in the total population. Thus there were two hundred and sixty or seventy agencies through the nation, and the agents with their salesmen made up a working force of from twelve to fifteen hundred men.

The higher purposes of this industrial empire, which the employees almost never referred to by name, as who should speak of the deity with coarse directness, but always with a just perceptible lowering and huskiness of the voice as "the Company"—these higher purposes were also beautifully simple. They were summed up in the famous utterance of the Great Man himself, Mr. Paul S. Appleton, III, who invariably repeated it every year as a peroration to his hour-long address before the assembled members of the sales organization at their national convention. Standing before them at the close of each year's session, he would sweep his arm in a gesture of magnificent command toward an enormous map of the United States of America that covered the whole wall behind him, and say:

"There's your market! Go out and sell them!"

What could be simpler and more beautiful than this? What could more eloquently indicate that mighty sweep of the imagination which has been celebrated in the annals of modern business under the name of "vision?" The words had the spacious scope and austere directness that have characterized the utterances of great leaders in every epoch of man's history. It is Napoleon speaking to his troops in Egypt: "Soldiers, from the summit of yonder pyramids, forty centuries look down upon you." It is Captain Perry: "We have met the enemy, and they are ours." It is Dewey at Manila Bay: "You may fire when ready, Gridley." It is Grant before Spottsylvania Court House: "I propose to fight it out on this line, if it takes all summer."

So when Mr. Paul S. Appleton, III, waved his arm at the wall and said: "There's your market! Go out and sell them!"—the assembled captains, lieutenants, and privates in the ranks of his sales organization knew that there were still giants in the earth, and that the age of romance was not dead.

True, there had once been a time when the aspirations of the Company had been more limited. That was when the founder of the institution, the grandfather of Mr. Paul S. Appleton, III, had expressed his modest hopes by saying: "I should like to see one of my machines in every store, shop, or business that needs one, and that can afford to pay for one." But the self-denying restrictions implicit in the founder's statement had long since become so out of date as to seem utterly mid-Victorian. Mr. David Merrit admitted it himself. Much as he hated to speak ill of any man, and especially the founder of the Company, he had to confess that by the standards of 1929 the old gentleman had lacked vision.

"That's old stuff now," said Mr. Merrit, shaking his head and winking at George, as though to take the curse off of his treason to the founder by making a joke of it. "We've gone way beyond that!" he exclaimed with pardonable pride. "Why, if we waited nowadays to sell a machine to someone who *needs* one, we'd get nowhere." He was nodding now at Randy, and speaking with the seriousness of deep conviction. "We don't wait until he *needs* one. If he says he's getting along all right without one, we make him buy one anyhow. We make him *see* the need, don't we, Randy? In other words, we *create* the need."

This, as Mr. Merrit went on to explain, was what is known in more technical phrase as "creative salesmanship" or "creating the market." And this poetic conception was the inspired work of one man—none other than the present head of the Company, Mr. Paul S. Appleton, III, himself. The idea had come to him in a single blinding flash, born full-blown like Pallas Athene from the head of Zeus, and Mr. Merrit still remembered the momentous occasion as vividly as if it had been only yesterday. It was at one of the meetings of the assembled parliaments of the Company that Mr. Appleton, soaring in an impassioned flight of oratory, became so intoxicated with the grandeur of his own vision that he stopped abruptly in the middle of a sentence and stood there as one entranced, gazing out dreamily into the unknown vistas of magic Canaan; and when he at least went on again, it was in a voice surcharged with quivering emotion:

"My friends," he said, "the possibilities of the market, now that we see how to create it, are practically unlimited!" Here he was silent for a moment, and Mr. Merrit said that the Great Man actually paled and seemed to stagger as he tried to speak, and that his voice faltered and sank to an almost inaudible whisper, as if he himself could hardly comprehend the magnitude of his own conception. "My friends—" he muttered thickly, and was seen to clutch the rostrum for support—"my friends—seen properly—" he whispered, and moistened his dry lips— "seen properly—the market we shall create being what it is—" his voice grew stronger, and the clarion words now rang forth— "there is no reason why one of our machines should not be in the possession of every man, woman, and child in the United States!" Then came the grand, familiar gesture to the map: "There's your market, boys! Go out and sell them!"

Henceforth this vision became the stone on which Mr. Paul S. Appleton, III, erected the magnificent office of the true church and living faith which was called "the Company." And in the service of this vision Mr. Appleton built up an organization which worked with the beautiful precision of a locomotive piston. Over the salesman was the agent, and over the agent was the district supervisor, and over the district supervisor was the district manager, and over the district manager was the general manager, and over the general manager was—if not God himself, then the next thing to it, for the agents and salesmen referred to him in tones of proper reverence as "P.S.A."

Mr. Appleton also invented a special Company Heaven known as the Hundred Club. Its membership was headed by P.S.A., and all the ranks of the sales organization were eligible, down to the humblest salesman. The Hundred Club was a social order, but it was also a good deal more than that. Each agent and salesman had a "quota"— that is to say, a certain amount of business which was assigned to him as the normal average of his district and capacity. A man's quota differed from another's according to the size of his territory, its wealth, and his own experience and ability. One man's quota would be sixty, another's eighty, another's ninety or one hundred, and if he was a district agent, his quota would be higher than that of a mere salesman. Each man, however, no matter how small or how large his quota might be, was eligible for membership in the Hundred Club, the only restriction being that he must average one hundred per cent of his quota. If he averaged more—if he got, say, one hundred and twenty per cent of his quota—there were appropriate honors and rewards, not only social but financial as well. One could be either high up or low down in the Hundred Club, for it had almost as many degrees of merit as the Masonic Order.

The unit of the quota system was "the point," and the point was forty dollars' worth of business. So if a salesman had a quota of eighty, this meant that he had to sell the products of the Federal Weight, Scales and Computing Company to the amount of at least $3200 every month, or almost $40,000 a year. The rewards were high. A salesman's commission was from fifteen to twenty per center of his sales; an agent's, from twenty to twenty-five percent. Beyond this were bonuses to be earned by achieving or surpassing his quota. Thus it was possible for an ordinary salesman in an average district to earn from $6000 to $8000 a year, while an agent could earn from $12,000 to $15,000, and even more if his district was an exceptionally good one.

So much for the rewards of Mr. Appleton's Heaven. But what would Heaven be if there were no Hell? So Mr. Appleton was forced by the logic of the situation to invent a Hell, too. Once a man's quota was fixed at any given point, the Company never reduced it. Moreover, if a salesman's quota was eighty points and he achieved it during a year, he must be prepared at the beginning of the new year to find that his quota had been increased to ninety points. One had to go onward and upward constantly, and the race was to the swift.

While it was quite true that membership in the Hundred Club was not compulsory, it was also true that Mr. Paul S. Appleton, III, was a theologian who, like Calvin, knew how to combine free will and predestination. If one did not belong to the Hundred Club, the time was not far distant when one would not belong to Mr. Appleton. Not to belong to it was, for agent or salesman, the equivalent of living on the other side of the railroad tracks. If one failed of admission to the Company Heaven, or if one dropped out, his fellows would begin to ask guardedly: "Where's Joe Klutz these days?" The answers would be vague, and in the course of time Joe Klutz would be spoken of no more. He would fade into oblivion. He was "no longer with the Company" ...

The last day of his week in Libya Hill, George had gone to the station to buy his return ticket and he stopped in at Randy's office a little before one o'clock to go home to lunch with him. The outer salesroom, with it shining stock of scales and computing machines imposingly arrayed on walnut pedestals, was deserted, so he sat down to wait. On one wall hung a gigantic colored poster. "August Was the Best Month in Federal History," it read. "*Make September a Better One! The Market's There, Mr. Agent. The Rest is Up to You!*"

Behind the salesroom was a little partitioned space which served Randy as an office. As George waited, gradually he became aware of mysterious sounds emanating from beyond the partition. First there was a rustle of heavy paper, as if the pages of a ledger were being turned, and occasionally there would be a quick murmur of hushed voices, confidential, ominous, interspersed with grunts and half-suppressed exclamations. Then all at once there were two loud bangs, as of a large ledger being slammed shut and thrown upon a desk or table, and after a moment's silence the voices rose louder, distinct, plainly audible. Instantly he recognized Randy's voice—low, grave, hesitant, and deeply troubled. The other voice he had never heard before.

But as he listened to that voice he began to tremble and grow white about the lips. For its very tone was a foul insult to human life, an ugly sneer whipped across the face of decent humanity, and as he realized that that voice, these words, were being used against his friend, he had a sudden blind feeling of murder in his heart. And what was so perplexing and so troubling was that this devil's voice had in it as well a curiously familiar note, as of someone he had known.

Then it came to him in a flash—it was Merrit speaking! The owner of that voice, incredible as it seemed, was none other than that plump, well-kept, jolly-looking man who had always been so full of hearty cheerfulness and good spirits every time he had seen him.

Now, behind that little partition of glazed glass and varnished wood, this man's voice had suddenly become fiendish. It was inconceivable, and as George listened he grew sick, as one does in some awful nightmare when he visions someone he knows doing some perverse and abominable act. But what was most dreadful of all was Randy's voice, humble, low, submissive, modestly entreating. Merrit's voice would cut across the air like a gob of rasping phlegm, and then Randy's voice—gentle, hesitant, deeply troubled—would come in from time to time in answer.

"Well, what's the matter? Don't you want the job?"

"Why—why, yes, you know I do. Dave—haw-w—" and Randy's voice lifted a little in a troubled and protesting laugh.

"What's the matter that you're not getting the business?"

"Why—haw-w!—" again the little laugh, embarrassed and troubled—"I *thought* I was—"

"Well, you're not!" that rasping voice cut in like a knife. "This district ought to deliver thirty per cent more business than you're getting from it, and the Company is going to have it, too—or else! You deliver or you go right out on your can! See? The Company doesn't give a damn about you! It's after the business! You've been around a long time, but you don't mean a damn bit more to the Company than anybody else! And you know what's happened to a lot of other guys who got to feeling they were too big for their job—don't you!"

"Why—why, yes, Dave—but—haw-w!" the little laugh again—"but-honestly, I never thought—"

"We don't give a damn what you never thought!" the brutal voice ripped in. "I've given you fair warning now! You get the business or out you go!"

The glazed glass door burst open violently and Merrit came striding out of the little partitioned office. When he saw George, he looked startled. Then he was instantly transformed. His plump and ruddy face became wreathed in smiles, and he cried out in a hearty tone:

"Well, well, well! Look who's here! If it's not the old boy himself!"

Randy had followed him out, and Merrit now turned and winked humorously at him, in the manner of a man who is carrying on a little bantering byplay:

"Randy," he said, "I believe George gets better looking from day to day. Has he broken any hearts yet?"

Randy tried to smile, grey-faced and haggardly.

"I bet you're burning them up in the Big Town," said Merrit, turning back to George. "And, say, I read that piece in the paper about your book. Great Stuff, son! We're all proud of you!"

He gave George a hearty slap on the back and turned away with an aid of jaunty readiness, picked up his hat, and said cheerfully:

"Well, what d'ya say, folks? What about one of Margaret's famous meals, out at the old homestead? Well, you can't hurt my feelings. I'm ready if you are. Let's go!"

And, smiling, ruddy, plump, cheerful, a perverted picture of amiable good will to all the world, he sauntered through the door. For a moment the two old friends just stood there looking at each other, white and haggard, with a bewildered expression in their eyes. In Randy's eyes there was also a look of shame. With that instinct for loyalty which was one of the roots of his soul, he said:

"Dave's a good fellow...You— you see, he's got to do these things...He—he's with the Company."

George didn't say anything. For as Randy spoke, and George remembered all that Merritt had told him about the Company, a terrific picture flashed through his mind. It was a picture he had seen in a gallery somewhere, portraying a long line of men stretching from the Great Pyramid to the very portals of great Pharaoh's house, and great Pharaoh stood with a thonged whip in his hand and applied it unmercifully to the bare back and shoulders of the man in front of him, who was great Pharaoh's chief overseer, and in the hand of the overseer was a whip of many tails which he unstintedly applied to the quivering back of the wretch before him, who was the chief overseer's chief lieutenant, and in the lieutenant's hand a whip of rawhide which he laid vigorously on the quailing body of his head sergeant, and in the sergeant's hand a wicked flail with which he belabored a whole company of groaning corporals, and in the hands of every corporal a knotted lash with which to whack a whole regiment of slaves, who pulled and hauled and bore burdens and toiled and sweated and built the towering structure of the pyramid.

So George didn't say anything. He couldn't. He had just found out something about life that he had not known before.

Discussion Question: Much of our way of life revolves around commercial transactions, such as buying and leasing goods, payment relationships, and financing: just consider how much time we spend shopping and obsessing over money. Some would say that we have created a society that is the envy of other countries, due to our limitless array of available products and extensions of credit; others would say that our lives are too dominated by commercial relations at the expense of family, community, and social justice. In the selection that you just read, Wolfe depicts antagonistic and pressured workplace relationships, all in the service of a Company that wants to sell the public a product it doesn't need. Is this an accurate portrayal of contemporary life? Does the Code put any brakes on such a way of life?

The Negotiable Cow
Sir Alan Herbert[4]

'Was the cow crossed?'

'No, your worship, it was an open cow.'

These and similar passages provoked laughter at Bow Street today when the Negotiable Cow Case was concluded.

Sir Joshua Hoot, K.C. (appearing for the Public Prosecutor): Sir Basil, these summonses, by leave of the court, are being heard together, an unusual but convenient arrangement.

The defendant, Mr. Albert Haddock, has for many months, in spite of earnest endeavors on both sides, been unable to establish harmonious relations between himself and the Collector of Taxes. The Collector maintains that Mr. Haddock should make over a large part of his earnings to the Government. Mr. Haddock replies that the proportion demanded is excessive, in view of the inadequate services or consideration which he himself has received from that Government. After an exchange of endearing letters, telephone calls, and even cheques, the sum demanded was reduced to fifty-seven pounds; and about this sum the exchange of opinions continued.

On the 31st of May the Collector was diverted from his respectable labors by the apparition of a noisy crowd outside his windows. The crowd, Sir Basil, had been attracted by Mr. Haddock, who was leading a large white cow of malevolent aspect. On the back and sides of the cow were clearly stenciled in red ink the following words:

4. A.P. Herbert, *Uncommon Law* (London: Methuen & Co, Ltd, 1972). Copyright 1935 by A. P. Herbert.

'To the London and Literary Bank, Ltd.

'Pay the Collector of Taxes, who is no gentleman, on Order, the sum of fifty-seven pounds (and may he rot!).

'£57/0/0

'ALBERT HADDOCK'

Mr. Haddock conducted the cow into the Collector's office, tendered it to the Collector in payment of income-tax and demanded a receipt.

Sir Basil String: Did the cow bear the statutory stamp?

Sir Joshua: Yes, a twopenny stamp was affixed to the dexter horn. The Collector declined to accept the cow, objecting that it would be difficult or even impossible to pay the cow into the bank. Mr. Haddock, throughout the interview, maintained the friendliest demeanor; and he now remarked that the Collector could endorse the cow to any third party to whom he owed money, adding that there must be many persons in that position. The Collector then endeavoured to endorse the cheque—

Sir Basil String: Where?

Sir Joshua: On the back of the cheque, Sir Basil, that is to say, on the abdomen of the cow. The cow, however, appeared to resent endorsement and adopted a menacing posture. The Collector, abandoning the attempt, declined finally to take the cheque. Mr. Haddock led the cow away and was arrested in Trafalgar Square for causing an obstruction. He has also been summoned by the Board of Inland Revenue for nonpayment of income-tax.

Mr. Haddock, in the witness-box, said that he had tendered a cheque in payment of income-tax, and if the Commissioners did not like his cheque they could do the other thing. A cheque was only an order to a bank to pay money to the person in possession of the cheque or a person named on the cheque. There was nothing in statute or customary law to say that an order must be written on a piece of paper of specified dimensions. A cheque, it was well known, could be written on a piece of notepaper. He himself had drawn cheques on the backs of menus, on napkins, on handkerchiefs, on the labels of wine-bottles; all these cheques had been duly honored by his bank and passed through the Bankers' Clearing House. He could see no distinction in law between a cheque written on a napkin and a cheque written on a cow. The essence of each document was a written order to pay money, made in the customary form and in accordance with statutory requirements as to stamps, etc. A cheque was admittedly not legal tender in the sense that it could not lawfully be refused; but it was accepted by custom as a legitimate form of payment. There were funds in his bank sufficient to meet the cow; the commissioners might not like the cow, but, the cow having been tendered, they were estopped from charging him with failure to pay. (Mr. Haddock here cited *Spowers v. The Strand Magazine, Lucas v. Finck,* and *Wadsworth v. The Metropolitan Water Board.*)

As to the action of the police, Mr. Haddock said it was a nice thing if in the heart of the commercial capital of the world a man could not convey a negotiable instrument down the street without being arrested. He had instituted proceedings against Constable Boot for false imprisonment.

Cross-examined as to motive, witness said that he had no cheque-forms available and, being anxious to meet his obligations promptly, had made use of the only material to hand. Later, he admitted that there might have been present in his mind a desire to make the Collector of Taxes look ridiculous. But why not? There was no law against deriding the income-tax.

Sir Basil String (after the hearing of further evidence): This case has at least brought to the notice of the Court a citizen who is unusual both in his clarity of mind and integrity of behavior. No thinking man can regard those parts of the Finance Acts which govern the income-tax with anything but contempt. There may be something to be said—not much—for taking from those who have inherited wealth a certain proportion of that wealth for the service of the State and the benefit of the poor and needy; and those who by their own ability, brains, industry, and exertion have earned money may reasonably be invited to surrender a small portion of it towards the maintenance of those public services by which they benefit, to wit, the Police, the Navy, the Army, the public sewers, and so forth. But to compel such individuals to bestow a large part of their earnings upon other individuals, whether by way of pensions, unemployment grants, or education allowances, is manifestly barbarous and indefensible. Yet this is the law. The original and only official basis of taxation was that individual citizens, in return for their money, received collectively some services from the State, the defence of their property and persons, the care of their health or the education of their children. All that has now gone. Citizen A, who has earned money, is commanded simply to give it to Citizens B, C, and D, who have not, and by force of habit this has come to be regarded as a normal and proper proceeding, whatever the comparative industry or merits of Citizens A, B, C, and D. To be alive has become a virtue, and the mere capacity to inflate the lungs entitled Citizen B to a substantial share in the laborious earnings of Citizen A. The defendant, Mr. Haddock, repels and resents this doctrine, but, since it has received the sanction of Parliament, he dutifully complies with it. Hampered by practical difficulties, he took the first steps he could to discharge his legal obligations to the State. Paper was not available, so he employed instead a favorite cow. Now, there can be nothing obscene, offensive, or derogatory in the presentation of a cow by one man to another. Indeed, in certain parts of our Empire the cow is venerated as a sacred animal. Payment in kind is the oldest form of payment, and payment in kind more often than not meant payment in cattle. Indeed, during the Saxon period, Mr. Haddock tell us, cattle were described as *viva pecunia*, or 'living money,' from their being received as payment on such occasions, at certain regulated prices. So that, whether the cheque was valid or not, it was impossible to doubt the validity of the cow; and whatever the Collector's distrust of the former it was at least his duty to accept the letter and credit Mr. Haddock's account with its value. But, as Mr. Haddock protested in his able argument, an order to pay is an order to pay, whether it is made on the back of an envelope or on the back of a cow. The evidence of the bank is that Mr. Haddock's account was in funds. From every point of view, therefore, the Collector of Taxes did wrong, by custom if not by law, in refusing to take the proffered animal, and the summons issued at his instance will be discharged.

As for the second charge, I hold again that Constable Boot did wrong. It cannot be unlawful to conduct a cow through the London streets. The horse, at the present time a much less useful animal, constantly appears in those streets without protest, and the motorcar, more unnatural and unattractive still, is more numerous than either animal. Much less can the cow be regarded as an improper or unlawful companion when it is invested (as I have shown) with all the dignity of a bill of exchange.

If people choose to congregate in one place upon the apparition of Mr. Haddock with a promissory cow, then Constable Boot should arrest the people, not Mr. Haddock. Possibly, if Mr. Haddock had paraded Cockspur Street with a paper cheque for one million pounds made payable to bearer, the crowd would have been as great, but that is not to say that Mr. Haddock would have broken the law. In my judgment Mr. Haddock has behaved throughout in the manner of a perfect knight, citizen, and taxpayer. The charge brought by the Crown is dismissed; and I hope with all my heart that in his action against Constable Boot Mr. Haddock will be successful. What is the next case, please?

Discussion Question: Does the Code provide a quick solution to the problem raised in this story, namely whether the cow was a negotiable instrument (see 3-104)?

Depositing The Junk Mail Check
Patrick Combs[5]

On May 19, 1995, I was one of thousands of people around the country who received a "junk mail" letter touting a get-rich-quick method for making $95,093.35 in just three weeks. That letter also came with a sample check for the same amount—$95,093.35. Everything about the check looked good except for the words "non-negotiable for cash" printed in the top right-hand corner. I look at the check and think, My God, it looks so real. The letter reads, "Patrick Combs, I expected to hear from you by now. Take a close look at the check above. It's just a sample of the money you could be receiving by now." I think, sample? Like a cookie sample at Mrs. Fields—it's a real cookie, but it's just a sample.

The letter went on: "We took in that amount in just three weeks. Other mail boxes have also made hundreds of thousands of dollars. In fact, your mail box, at 326 Howard Street, could be soon stuffed full of checks in varying amounts and free merchandise. Now I've written to you several times before about an exciting new money making opportunity. The one that said 95,093.35 in just three weeks. The same one that was featured on TV! And frankly I'm surprised I haven't heard from you yet. Patrick, I know what you must be thinking, 'Is this for real?' Let me assure you, it is very real."

---

5. Patrick Combs, *The $95,093.35 Adventure*, http://www.goodthink.com. Copyright 1995 by Patrick Combs. Reprinted by permission of the author.

That's all I needed to know to take this check and deposit it into my ATM.

Now, I didn't believe it was a real check, but it was fun, like putting Monopoly money into the bank. And I knew my bank would never cash the check, especially since I didn't even sign on the back. I walked home picturing a bank teller opening my deposit envelope and chuckling at the sight of the ridiculously large, and obviously bogus check. I fully expected that on Monday morning someone from my bank would call and say, "Mr. Combs, the check you deposited on Friday wasn't real."

On Monday when they didn't call, I figured they were mailing the check back to me and I forgot about the whole thing.

Then two days later, while I was withdrawing $40, my ATM produced a receipt that told me my balance was over one hundred thousand dollars. Suddenly I remembered the $95,093.35 deposit. My heart leapt out of my chest. I ran all the way home (the most exercise I'd gotten in months!). As soon as I got in, I called a friend and told her what had happened. She made a quick phone call to her own bank and called me back. "It's standard policy to credit your account for any money you deposit, but it's only a credit. You can't touch the money unless the check clears."

Of course. It was just a matter of days before the bank would erase the credit and return my account to a mere $5,000. I figured it would be the week of my life when I had a one hundred thousand dollar bank balance. And I took full advantage of it by printing out lots of bank balance statements, and sharing them with my friends, i.e., "Need my phone number? I'll just write it here on the back of my ATM receipt." Without fail, it would always prompt a great conversation.

It was also very entertaining to call my twenty-four hour banking line, and listen to my bank balance. I did it twice, three times, four times a day. To my surprise, it remained at over a hundred grand, all week long. I was thinking, that check should have been bounced by now. Friday morning, I went to my bank, a branch of First Interstate, approached a teller, and posed this question: "If I need a cashier's check for $70,000 later this afternoon, do I have the funds available?" The teller typed my account number into her computer. "Yes," she said, "the money is available." I said, "Are you sure there is not a warning sign, a flashing light, an asterisk or something?" She assured me there wasn't.

I got out of the bank fast. I felt supercharged with possibility and shock.

From that moment until the next Wednesday, when I boarded a plane for a four-day career-counseling conference in Orlando (I make my living as an author and speaker addressing career success), $95,093.35 was available for withdrawal from my account. My close friends and I contemplated, for fun, all the possibilities a hundred grand afforded. "To leave the country or not to leave: that is the question."

I knew that the money was going to be taken out of my account, and each day I figured it would happen tomorrow. I boarded my flight to Orlando confident—and glad, really—that in all likelihood the money would be gone upon my return. It had already possessed my thoughts for a week.

On Monday, the day after my return, I called for my account balance. Five thousand and something dollars was what I expected to hear. What I did hear was over $100,000.

What was happening? Two weeks and that money was still sitting in my account.

"It will be gone tomorrow," I kept telling myself for the next five days. Then on Friday, exactly three weeks since I had deposited the sample check, I again returned to the bank. I approached a bank teller at the special Customer Service window, and I sternly stated, "I recently deposited $95,000 and I don't want to spend any of the money if there is the possibility of the check being returned. How long should I wait?"

The teller keyed in my account number. Then she said, "$95,093.35 was deposited on May 21. You're safe to spend that money now because that check can no longer be returned. Depositors are protected by a law that says checks cannot be returned after ten business days."

I couldn't believe my ears. I couldn't believe my luck. I couldn't believe what was happening.

On my way out of the bank, I grabbed every brochure and pamphlet that vaguely implied it might contain the law she had just referenced, and I went home and read voraciously.

My reading didn't reveal the law I was looking for. Quickly, I learned that bank brochures don't tell you your rights; they tell you all the bank's rights. And banks have a lot of rights. At the end of one of the brochures, however, I found a reference that said, "For more information, contact the Office of Thrift Supervision (O.T.S.)." I called the O.T.S. and a man answered the phone. I gave my first name only and give him a quick synopsis. He treated my story with a cool intrigue. He told me that the ten-day law the teller had mentioned was known as the "Midnight Deadline." But he suggested that the more important legal question had to do with "negotiability." He wondered if the check I deposited was a true negotiable instrument. He said, "The banking law book, Brady's, has specific criteria that a check has to match in order to qualify as a legal negotiable instrument. I'm not sure what they are, but if the check you deposited was actually a negotiable instrument, that would explain why your bank passed it."

Within three hours I was on my way to the Hastings Law Library and to the book *Brady on Bank Checks: The Law of Bank Checks.*

Soon I knew why law students always looked so beat and tired. I didn't know how I was going to find anything in the monstrous tome in front of me.

Then my eyes caught sight of a small, pocket-sized book titled *Negotiable Instruments and Check Collection*, a guide for laymen. And plain as day, it listed nine criteria for a negotiable instrument. Read for yourself what I read, and I believe you'll yell out loud just as I did when I came to the very last word:

1. Must be in writing.

2. Signed by maker or drawer.

3. Promise or order...A check usually meets the requirement because the drawee's name is printed and encoded on the face of the instrument.

4. Unconditional.

5. Order to pay money.

6. Must be a fixed amount.

7. Payable on demand or at a definite time.

8. Payable to order or to bearer.

9. No other undertaking or instruction.

The final requirement of negotiability is that beyond the maker's order the instrument must not contain 'any other undertaking or instruction'... The opposite issue is whether or not the parties can use a form that is a negotiable instrument and avoid negotiability by declaring, on the instrument, that it is not negotiable. The answer is "yes, except for a check."

This was one book I wanted to steal from the library (but didn't). The get-rich-quick company had accidentally designed a real check, and I had deposited it!

Discussion Question: Is this legit? Give an answer using Article 3, Article 4, and/or the federal regulations, if necessary. Warning: this question is harder than it seems! You might begin by asking whether Combs was correct in concluding that the check qualifies as a negotiable instrument. (P.S. This is a true story, included here because it makes for a great narrative. Ultimately, Combs returned the money, but he still maintains that the money belonged to him, not to the bank, which was First Interstate).

Chapter Ten

Concluding Assessment of the Code

This chapter brings together diverse opinions about the Code as a whole. In the first selection, my students over the past several years give their anonymous opinions of the Code; the responses range from the insightful to the insipid. In the second piece, Grant Gilmore (an important figure in the Code project) concludes that the Code fell prey to competing interest groups, resulting in a "compromise solution which satisfied no one." Finally, Professors J.J. White and Robert Summers, authors of the most influential treatise on the Code, disagree on whether the Code is a success story. Summers expresses scepticism about the Code project, but White claims that we are better off with the Code than we would be without it.

My own opinion: the Code is deeply ambiguous. It represents the best and worst of American law, and reproduces (but does not resolve, even tentatively) conflicts which plague the larger society. It was enacted to make the law simpler (see 1-102), yet it is frustratingly complicated. Llewellyn intended to put all the laws of commercial transactions in one location, yet the Code has been pre-empted by federal and state regulations and interpreted in so many ways that the diligent researcher must consult a wealth of material beyond the Code itself. At a deeper level the Code replicates but cannot solve the conflicting interests of parties to commercial transactions, so it professes freedom of contract (1-102(3)), but disallows specific provisions that the parties might reach freely (9-602); it creates implied warranties to protect consumers from merchants (2-314) and then allows the warranties to be disclaimed (2-316)—it gives with one hand and takes away with the other. But perhaps these conflicts (between rich and poor, the powerful and the powerless, entities and persons, businesses and consumers) are so deep that no code could negotiate them. The end result is a document that is less likely to inspire respect than to generate frustration. But what is the alternative? We cannot return to the common law, nor to the uniform laws approach which predated the Code, and even federal enactment raises serious problems. Perhaps we are so accustomed to the Code that we fail to appreciate the improvement that it has wrought, so maybe Professor

White is correct that the operative question that we should be asking is, 'Are we better off with the Code than without it?' Most people would answer that question with a 'Yes.'

Student Responses to the Question: "What is Your Opinion of the UCC?"[1]

"I think that the Code provides a basic structure for commercial transactions to take place and provides all parties involved with a basic idea of what to expect if they do not comply with the provisions. However, I do believe that they could very well accomplish this in a far less convoluted manner. There seems to be too much contradiction and that makes it difficult to follow at times."

"The Code is like a maze to me. Sometimes there is a way out, yet at other times there is a dead end. For example, many definitions, such as what is "reasonable," tell you nothing. Also, often times you have to shuffle between too many provisions to get an answer. The Code needs to do a better job of making things more clear and easy to understand."

"The Code is a big scary thing. It is not as bad when you actually get down to it, but it is imposing at first. It is also difficult to know where to go for each individual issue. It may be better if there was a different way of organizing it. It does, however, give you an answer for many problems that come up; it is more concrete than just common law jurisprudence."

"I feel that the basic objective of the Code, a centralized, exhaustive and uniform source of commercial law is laudable and it is successful in many respects; however, too often a practitioner is forced to look for answers from external sources like cases and federal statutes. This undermines the Code's intent, and can lead to confusion on behalf of the parties to a transaction."

"I found the Official Comment sections of the Code more useful than the actual sections themselves. The Code would be more useful to me if it defined and explained in greater details the terms and reasons for a section."

"Of course the Code is not perfect, but in covering such a wide parameter of topics, could it ever be? After spending a semester getting

---

1. Students, University of Miami School of Law and Florida Coastal School of Law.

used to it, I feel that there is a system to it. Although there are gaps, you can make your way through it and provide adequate structure to any commercial transaction. Therefore I think ultimately it serves its purpose."

"I must say that when I first started to read the Code I hated it. But now that we have thoroughly studied the Code, I can safely say that I still hate it. It is ambiguous, impractical and extremely hard to follow. Somebody needs to write a UCC for dummies. I must admit the Official Comments are somewhat helpful but not enough."

"I don't think the Code is practical. It took me an entire semester to even get a grasp of the Code. The average business person who will be using the Code probably doesn't have a legal education. Therefore, they will be bound by something they don't understand. This is harmful to business people, especially small business owners who can't afford to retain lawyers. Even if a business person understands the Code, they can do everything the Code tells them to do and still get screwed. This is partly because the Code can be preempted by adverse federal laws. This is also partly because of the way the Code is written. For example, someone who took the right steps to perfect their security interest could still lose their interest to a later creditor under certain perverse rules of the Code."

"The Code works, if you know what works means. However, the Code, the UCC as it is properly called, is a maze waiting to be solved. Until then, U.(Professor Litowitz) will always demand readers to C.(see) that they need to C.(see) another Code section to make the Code really work."

"I like the Code. I feel that the answers to your legal questions can be answered in the Code. Granted, you may not get the exact, in detail, answer; however, you are given a guiding voice. If this area of the law was controlled by judicial mandate via cases, it would be too frustrating to practice. The Code is not perfect, but, I feel that it is a workable compromise. Honestly, I wish that other areas of the law had a guiding force such as the Code. The Code allows someone who has mastered its themes to effectively argue any point."

"The Code bites! It is completely confusing. There are too many provisions which open up too much room for errors. It needs to be more clear cut. The Comments and the rules themselves seem to conflict. Comments should assist a straightforward rule rather than complicate a vague one."

Discussion Question: Although some of these student responses seem flippant or simplistic, they were given anonymously, and therefore seem heartfelt. Let's hear *your* brief assessment of the Code! In particular, should there be a Code in the first place, and should it be organized in the current fashion?

Assessment of the Uniform Commercial Code
Grant Gilmore[2]

The Code was jointly sponsored by the National Conference of Commissioners on Uniform State Laws (which had acquired a de facto monopoly on commercial law codification) and the American Law Institute (which had completed the Restatement project but was, like any organization, reluctant to shut up shop and go out of business). The Conference had access to the state legislatures; the Institute had access to money; at the relevant time William Schnader, a Philadelphia lawyer, held high office in both organizations and is credited with having arranged their unlikely collaboration. While the memberships overlapped to some extent, the Conference was predominantly made up of small-town lawyers; the typical Institute member was a senior partner in a prestigious law firm or a federal judge or a law school dean. Most Commissioners and most members of the Institute were conservatives—not only in politics but in jurisprudence.

There is a comforting irony in the fact that the Conference and Institute not only chose Karl Llewellyn as principal draftsman (or Chief Reporter) for the Code but succeeded in living with him for fifteen years on terms of mutual respect and amity. Llewellyn in the 1930s had become the symbol of the academic revolt against Langdellianism and orthodoxy. He was flamboyant both in his personality and his prose style. He must have seemed, to most members of both Conference and Institute, unsound. On the other hand, Llewellyn had been a devoted member of the Conference for many years and had become the Conference's principal draftsman in commercial law matters. He was also, beyond question, the preeminent academic author-

---

2. Grant Gilmore, The Ages of American Law (New Haven: Yale University Press, 1977). Copyright 1977 by Yale University Press. Reprinted by permission.

ity on sales law (which was the starting point for the Code project). In all probability, Llewellyn thought that he could persuade his employers to adopt his own theories. In turn, the people who controlled the Conference and Institute thought that they could make use of Llewellyn's drafting skills and encyclopedic knowledge of the law, while reserving the power to veto any excesses toward which their unpredictable Chief Reporter might seek to lead them.

On the whole and in the long run the conservatives or traditionalists had their way. Llewellyn's proposals for a radical restructuring of the law—as, for example, in distinguishing between the standards applicable to "merchants" and those applicable to non-merchants—survived the early drafts only in an attenuated, watered down, almost meaningless form. Provisions which would have notably increased the liability of manufacturers for their defective goods were simply deleted from the later drafts. Not only the substance but the style of the Code changed dramatically as the drafting process continued. Llewellyn himself had the concept of what he called a "case law code"—by which he meant a statute whose principal function would be to abrogate obsolete rules, thus leaving the courts free to improvise new rules to fit changing conditions and novel business practices. Llewellyn's code, as he conceived it, would have abolished the past without attempting to control the future. That jurisprudential approach did not satisfy the groups of practicing lawyers who participated in the project and whose influence increased as the drafting approached the final stages. These lawyers had perhaps become uneasily aware of mounting indications of a new style of judicial activism. At all events they insisted on a tightly drawn statute, designed to control the courts and compel decisions. To a considerable degree, they got what they wanted.

The Code in its final form can best be described as a compromise solution which satisfied no one. Llewellyn had recruited a drafting staff which was composed mostly of younger law professors whose own ideas about law had been greatly influenced by Llewellyn and the other Realists. Sharing Llewellyn's views, they produced drafts which reflected his own pluralism and anti-conceptualism. Those drafts were largely rewritten by practitioners whose instinctive approach to law was more conventional. Even so, the Code, as rewritten, retained more than mere traces of the earlier approach, both in substance and in style. It testifies to the fundamental cleavage which, by the 1940s, had overtaken the legal profession in this country.

It was the curious fate of the Code, a 1940s statute, not to have been widely enacted until the 1960s. In the 1950s the legal establishment which controlled the bar associations (and had great influence with the bankers' associations) opposed the Code and was successful in preventing its enactment. In the 1960s the same people who had fought the Code ten years earlier had reversed their field and were counted among its most vigorous supporters. A plausible reason for this reversal is that during the 1950s the courts, in a surge of activism, had themselves been rewriting much of the law. The Code, which in the 1940s had seemed much too "liberal" to its conservative critics, had by the 1960s become an almost nostalgic throwback to an earlier period. The final irony in the Code project was that its eventual "success" (that is, its enactment) can well be taken as an attempt by the most conservative elements in the bar to turn the clock back.

Discussion Question: Do you agree with Gilmore's characterization of the Code as a compromise, a sort of watered down version of Karl Llewellyn's original plan for an open-ended, flexible, consumer-friendly statute? Think about the warranty provisions (Sections 2-312 to 2-315) and the ability to disclaim warranties (2-316), and then ask yourself whether the Code is pro-consumer, pro-business, or is a compromise that satisfies neither group.

Uniform Commercial Code Romanticism (and Realism)
James J. White and Robert S. Summers[3]

In its early days, the Uniform Commercial Code was put forward as the grandest achievement of all time in the history of private statute law making. One of your co-authors (Summers) wishes to close this general introduction with some brief reflections on the ethos that prevailed in the 1950's when many of us first laid eyes on the Code's Official Text—an ethos that continues to prevail today in many quarters.

The ethos includes four main tenets. First, it is possible (more or less) to put all (or nearly all) of commercial law into a comprehensive

---

3. James J. White and Robert S. Summers, Uniform Commercial Code: Secured Transactions 21–22 (St. Paul: West Group, 2000). Reprinted with permission of the West Group.

code, and if that is done, the law will stay there, too. Second, if the law is put into a code (a well-drafted one, of course) then its generally precise text will greatly reduce uncertainty, enhance predictability, and diminish the volume of legal disputes. Third, if the law is put into a code, and all the states adopt it, then we will have a uniform body of commercial law among the several states (all fifty of them). Fourth, with all the law in a code (the right kind of code, of course), this code will be adaptable to change, and frequent amendment will not be necessary (let alone proposed).

One may call this ethos "Uniform Commercial Code Romanticism." In choosing that appellation, one thinks not of the traditional contrasts between the classical and the romantic in literature and the arts. Rather, one intends the less sophisticated and perhaps more familiar dictionary meaning of the word "romantic," namely that which is "fanciful, impractical, unrealistic, or excessively idealistic."

Enough facts are now in, and the truth is that all four of the foregoing tenets are either false or fanciful. It is neither possible nor desirable to put all (or even nearly all) commercial law into a code. And it hardly true that once law is put into a code, it will stay there. Indeed, today, some Code sections are little more than elaborate indexing systems—mere "ways" into the cases.

In addition, the Code may not have reduced uncertainty, enhanced predictability, or diminished the volume of disputes.

Furthermore, with fifty judiciaries at work, uniformity is simply not attainable on anything like the scale that the Code drafters originally envisioned. On many issues under Article Nine there are now major conflicts of authority. Yet Article Nine is as tightly drawn as any Code article.

Finally, the process of amendment continues apace, not least because some of the founding romanticists simply have never been able to leave the Code text alone, even for a moment. Indeed some of them presumably believe that there are simply no costs whatever attendant upon changes in the Official Text. In fact, these costs are considerable. Indeed, the continuing stream of "official" amendments alone accounts for much of today's lack of uniformity in the text.

Your other author (White) believes that the romantic ideals that Summers lists have been have been achieved to a much greater extent than Summers or others will concede. If one puts himself in the position of a lawyer who is attempting to resolve a commercial law problem for a client in 1938 on the one hand and in 2000 on the other, would anyone doubt that the lawyer in 2000 would find the law more uniform, more certain, more precise and more sensible? Only one who had been embarrassed by his earlier excesses of romanticism would deny such was the case.

Discussion Question: Are you a 'Code Romantic' who believes that the Code fulfills its basic mandate of clarity, uniformity, and modernization (1-102(2)), or are you a 'Code Realist' who sees the Code as a noble project that has fallen short of its intended goals?

Index